Safari as a Way of Life

Liberté Egalité Safari

chronicle books · san francisco

DAN ELDON

SAFARI AS A
WAY OF LIFE

BY JENNIFER NEW

Library of Congress Cataloging-in-Publication Data
New, Jennifer.
Dan Eldon : safari as a way of life / by Jennifer New.
p. cm.
ISBN 978-0-8118-7091-7 (Hardcover)
ISBN 978-1-4521-0207-8 (Library edition)
1. Eldon, Dan, 1970–1993. 2. Photojournalists—England—Biography.
3. Photojournalists—United States—Biography. 4. Africa—Description
and travel. I. Title.
TR140.E38N475 2011
770.92—dc22
[B]
2010051426

Book design by Kristine Brogno.
and McGuire Barber Design.
Typeset in Whitney.

Manufactured through Asia Pacific Offset by Power Printing, Heyuan,
China, in July 2011.

10 9 8 7 6 5 4 3 2 1

This product conforms to CPSIA 2008.

Chronicle Books LLC
680 Second Street
San Francisco, California 94107

www.chronicleteen.com

IMAGE CREDITS
Every effort has been made to trace copyright holders. If any unintended omissions have been
made, Chronicle Books would be pleased to add appropriate acknowledgments in future editions.

All photographs, illustrations, documents, and removable facsimiles are courtesy of the Estate
of Dan Eldon, except as noted: Page 19, 20, 21: photos © Kathy Eldon; Page 58: photo © Kathy
Eldon; Page 99, 106: photos © Marte Rambourg; Page 129: photos © Kathy Eldon; Page 131:
far right photo © Yannis Behrakis; Page 164, 165: top photos © Kathy Eldon; Page 165: bottom
photo: © Njoroge; Page 166: photo of Kathy speaking © Reuters; Page 168–169: photos © Kat
Fowler; Page 170: photo © Donatella Lorch; Page 171: Left photo © Joey Borgogna, right photo
© J. Nichola Graydon; Page 172: photos © Guillaume Bonne; Page 173: left photo © Kathy Eldon,
right photo © Tim LaPage; Page 174: photo © Kathy Eldon; Page 175: photos © Mike Eldon;
Page 176: photo © Jason Russell; Page 177: photos © Micah Wesley; Page 178–179: photos in
order from left to right ©: Eiji Shimizu, Hayden Bixby, Ryan Bixby, Amy Eldon Turteltaub, Marte
Rambourg, Elinor Tatum, Jeff Gettleman.

This book is for Dan's nieces and nephews, his cousins' children, the children of the STA gang and his ISK friends, as well as for my own children. In short, it is for those who will never know him but may be inspired by his journey. -J.N.

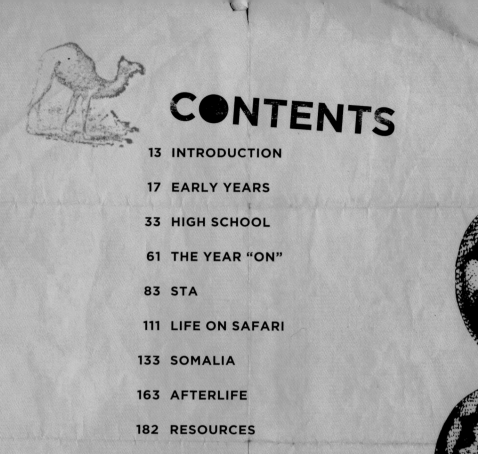

CONTENTS

INTRODUCTION

"Is that your son?" The woman sitting next to me on the plane gestures to my laptop and the photo of a young man that fills the screen. I suppose I am old enough—Dan was about twenty when the photo was taken—but it's impossible for me to think of him that way. If Dan were alive, he'd be about my age.

"Good looking kid," the woman adds. She's right. In fact, it's one of the first things people say about Dan Eldon. They take in his image—the long face, the dark brown eyes—and almost universally declare him handsome or beautiful.

I first encountered Dan in a San Francisco bookstore in 1997. He was staring down at me from the front cover of a book of his artwork that had been recently published. "I dare you to open it," he seemed to be saying. How could I resist?

A half hour later, I was smitten. Most people who spend any time with that book, *The Journey Is the Destination,* come away with a similar reaction, as well as a deep curiosity about the young man behind the images. The art is so dense, the colors so saturated; the emotions, which range from exuberance to anger, love, and grief, shoot off the pages. You are filled not just with appreciation but with questions: *Where was he when he made this? Who is that girl who keeps reappearing? How did he know all of these people—these totally gorgeous people? How did he do so much at such a young age?* And then, when you discover that he's no longer alive, you just wonder, *How? Why?*

Less than a year after that encounter, I met his mom, Kathy, at a museum where she was opening an exhibit of his work. In "The World of Dan"—as I jokingly refer to it—synchronicity rules, and my meeting with Kathy was no different. It turns out that she grew up in a mid-sized city in Iowa, just a half hour from where I live. I'd seen an ad that she would be speaking, and when I stayed after the event to introduce myself and give her the business card that I'd just had made, she immediately embraced my idea of building a Web site about Dan. That project gradually morphed into a biography, which brought me to her home in Los Angeles. I spent countless hours looking through Dan's journals and talking with Kathy and her daughter, Amy.

During the year that I wrote the biography, *Dan Eldon: The Art of Life*, I interviewed nearly a hundred people. In addition to some of his closest friends and his immediate family, I talked to Dan's high school art teacher, a journalist who roomed with him in Mogadishu, several ex-girlfriends, his summer camp counselor, and a man who was with him the day he died. What nearly all of them told me was that they still thought of Dan often—sometimes daily—and that he had changed their lives.

Was this just grief talking? Many people choose to remember the best about friends and relatives after their deaths. Those who are especially talented take on a larger-than-life quality—the James Dean effect, if you will. There is undoubtedly some of this going on with Dan's memory. And yet, he clearly had a very strong influence on people during his life, too.

"He made you feel like he had the high beams focused just on you," one friend recalled about what it was like to talk to Dan. Women remembered how beautiful he made them feel with his slightly flirtatious manner and his ability to listen, not to mention his habit of photographing them. A high school classmate who'd had a terrible stutter said Dan was the first person who'd ignored that and, instead, focused on his skill as an artist. Many people remembered Dan as colorblind—not literally but metaphorically. He saw all people, no matter their race, ethnicity, or income level, as equal; each was a potential friend. In Kenya, where he grew up, there were a lot of tightly drawn lines between races, countries of origin, tribes, and levels of wealth. Dan was oblivious to all this. One of his girlfriends was a Kikuyu princess and the granddaughter of the first president of Kenya. Another came from a single-parent home in the Midwest.

Dan would have been exceptional based solely on his accomplishments. Born in 1970 in London, he moved to Nairobi with his family when he was seven. Together, they traveled around eastern and northern Africa, as well as much of Europe. When he was old enough, Dan traveled on his own, first hitchhiking and later taking the Land Rover he bought with money from the education fund his grandparents had established. He eventually visited more than forty countries.

During his sophomore year in high school, Dan's entrepreneurial skills fully emerged when he held a series of dances for a classmate who needed open-heart surgery. At the same time, he started selling his Maasai friend Kipenget's jewelry around Nairobi. Two years after graduation, in 1990, he led a group of teenagers from Kenya to a refugee camp in Malawi where they delivered the $20,000 they'd raised in order to build wells.

All of it got recorded in his journals. He began the journals—8½-by-11-inch blank books that Dan filled with photographs, drawings, and scraps picked up on explorations—when he was fifteen, for a class assignment. They became the perfect place to keep the art he generated.

Like many kids, Dan had been an avid artist as a child, but unlike many kids, he never stopped drawing. By his early teens, he was regularly carrying a camera, a gift from his parents. He built a darkroom in his bedroom and started photographing the girls he was dating. After high school, he interned at a fashion magazine. The journals exploded at this time, as he learned more about design and had access to a new treasure chest of tools, including a color photocopier. Almost entirely self-trained, he started selling his photographs at a young age. He sometimes took photos to accompany his mother's articles for local newspapers and magazines. In 1991, when he arrived in Somalia, experiencing the civil war and famine there firsthand, he was quickly able to get a job as a freelance photographer, first for Kenya's largest newspaper and then for Reuters, an international news agency.

It was in Somalia that Dan died; he was part of a group of journalists who were killed while on the job. Dan's family, understandably, wanted to find ways to keep his memory alive.

His mother published his journals; his father set up a leadership training center for kids in Nairobi; his sister made a documentary about war correspondents.

Now, nearly twenty years after his death, Dan is much more than a memory; he's become a force. People discover his art, learn about his story, and go on their own journeys. Hundreds of thousands of people have been touched by Dan at this point, although most have never met him. Micah Wesley, for instance, encountered Dan during a high school journalism class. Her teacher used his work and the story of what he'd done in Somalia to inspire her students with the impact journalists can have. A few years later, Micah met Kathy Eldon and started working for a nonprofit that helped Liberian refugees. She also got involved with the student group Invisible Children. "Dan was the inspiration and source of both groups," she said, adding that she wants to eventually start her own organization and be able to tell people that Dan is the source.

This book is yet another telling of Dan's story, a chance for you to encounter the source of his art and unique approach to living. Use it as a roadmap, an inspiration to set a course for your own safari.

I have grown up in Africa

EARLY YEARS

1970–1984

Dan's life *really* began at seven. That's when he and his family moved to Kenya.

For seven years, he'd grown up in London—with drab buildings, paved roads, stores that opened on time, neatly trimmed gardens, and rain. Suddenly, there was a brilliant sun that was occasionally interrupted by three-minute deluges. On the streets, women sold vegetables and fruit displayed on wooden crates from little stalls. Cars and vans careened through the streets with extra passengers hanging on to their sides. There was a cacophony of sounds: a call to prayer outside a mosque, monkeys chattering, horns blaring, children singing. Whereas in England, it hadn't always been easy, especially to a young child, to tell rich from poor, now there were ghettos that covered many city blocks. Huts made from scavenged tin and cardboard stood within shouting distance of mansions with tennis courts and swimming pools.

From the beginning, Dan embraced his new country. He loved the extremes of Kenya, its verve and honesty. For the rest of his life, he would call it home.

Dan 1978

Dan was born in suburban London on September 18, 1970, to an American mother and a British father. Mike and Kathy met during the summer of 1967 when Mike had an internship in Iowa. They were set up on a blind date—but a double date and to different people. A year and a half later they were married, and moved to London. As though to compensate for the grayness of his surroundings, his young parents painted his room lemon yellow and built him a scooter and an indoor playground complete with a slide. His mother, Kathy, presciently bound and decorated little books in which to record family drawings and poetry. She thought his crib looked like a cage, so she lined it with postcards and pictures from magazines.

Dan's two extended families were very different. Dan's father, Mike, came from a Jewish family who had immigrated to London from Israel when Mike was a toddler. Mike's father was a businessman, who was also an amateur artist. Dan's mother's family, the Knapps, were Methodists, business and philanthropic leaders of their small Midwestern city. They were great travelers, visiting China and Moscow before relations with the U.S. thawed. Eventually, character traits from both families became obvious in Dan.

By the time Amy was born in 1974, London was losing its charm for the family. The suburbs bored Kathy, and she worried about her children growing up there. It was too gray, she thought, too quiet and polite. Soon enough, the monotony was disrupted in the form of a job offer. Mike was given a two-year stint in the East Africa office of a computer company. They were moving to Nairobi.

ABOVE: Kathy, Dan, and Mike in London, 1971.

From the beginning, Dan never wanted for things to look at.

—KATHY ELDON

ABOVE: Dan in London, age two.

Kenya circa 1977 was a safe and stable country. With its perfect weather—mid 70s and no humidity—and impressive game parks, it was popular with tourists. Nairobi, which had long been considered the capital of East Africa, had a strong expatriate community of wildlife researchers, business people, diplomats, and others who came through a year or two. Others were the descendants of British colonists who had arrived in the late 1800s and early 1900s for the vast and inexpensive farmland. Some of them had become protectors of Kenya's heritage and were active in politics and social programs.

Like many before, the Eldons fell in love with Kenya and decided to stay long term, soon plunging into Nairobi society. They became friends with the Leakeys, a legendary family of paleoanthropologists—as well as with politicians, journalists, and artists. Philip Leakey took Dan and Amy along with his own kids on outings into the bush. He described taking off and hitchhiking to South Africa when he was a teenager, not telling his parents where he was until the trip was well under way.

Kathy took a series of jobs. As a host for a tourist company, she entertained groups of Americans and Europeans at her home. She organized a celebration of Kenyan culture at the National Museum of Kenya and became a restaurant reviewer for Nairobi's biggest newspaper. In addition to work, Mike was active with Rotary and local politics.

The family's cook, William, was as much a friend and caretaker for Dan and Amy as he was a cook, often meeting them after school

and making snacks. He called Dan "Britishy," short for the British High Commissioner, and when Amy was grumpy he called her "Denfenzi," for the Minister of Defense. They called him *mjomba,* or uncle. The affection was mutual. When William and his wife, who lived more than a day's drive away from Nairobi, had twins, they named them Dan and Amy.

Though Dan and Amy Eldon were not twins, they were much closer than many brothers and sisters. The move to Africa cemented their relationship. In a new place, without easy distractions, they had to rely on each other for entertainment. They became good friends with each other's closest friends, too—Dan with Marilyn and Lara, and Amy with Lengai.

Dinner parties were the norm at the house, many of them spontneous. Kathy would meet

ABOVE: Dan with Amy on the edge of the Great Rift Valley.

F AFRICA

COBRAS
MAMBAS
CROCODILES
TORTOISES

people during the day and bring them home at night to a feast of anything that could be put together. Food was not the point; in fact, seafood curry, sometimes burnt, was often on the menu.

There were nearly as many houseguests as there were visitors for dinner. "We would come home from school to discover someone we'd never seen before sleeping in our bed," recalls Amy. "The only way to find out who they were was to check the tags on their suitcase."

The family's home was sprawling; it was actually three dwellings strung together. Dan had his own quarters away from the main house, complete with a small kitchen and bathroom. He covered his bedroom walls with a collection of spears and daggers, military regalia, dried snake skins, an elaborate feathered Maasai headdress, masks, and ostrich eggs. It was his studio and retreat.

From a young age, Dan had charm and the striking ability to talk to anyone, no matter

> I was talking to Kathy while she cooked when I realized that she was putting dishwashing liquid in the curry. When I pointed it out, she just said, "Blast! Well, no one will notice!" and threw in more curry powder.
>
> —TARA FITZGERALD, CHILDHOOD FRIEND

A team of frog researchers pitched their tents in the garden for a number of weeks. An American actor woke the household up with his morning voice exercises. Kathy and a novelist started working on a book together, and the man stayed for months until it was done. An Australian photographer came for a few nights, enchanting Dan and Amy with her travel stories, then spiked a high fever and stayed for six weeks longer after she was diagnosed with hepatitis.

their background or age. Even so, he would become overloaded now and then and seek out time alone. Eventually, this would mean taking *matatus*—privately owned vans that serve as public transit—out of the city into rural areas. But first it meant the roof: he'd hoist himself up on a drainpipe, unfurl a sleeping bag, and spend the night in relative silence and total darkness.

imagine a world without wheels or containers

My God!!

We gave a party tonight. The rice
and fish were terrible but everyone ate
them anyway. The guests were, David
Siberstein and his wife. He is the
Presidents doctor. The ex editor for 'Drum'
magazine, the south African based
political magazine. Not for the white
side. Lengai and his mother came
with an a white hunter who is staying
with them. Alan Meijr, a U.S. Army
doctor (Major) was also there

Zebra on Athi plains

24

Samburu warrior compares head gear.

KENYA AS INSPIRATION

Dan collected stories about Kenya's rich history. A land that contains at least eight different ethnic groups, it was a British colony from 1885 until its independence in 1963. Dan often poked fun at the uptight Brits who insisted on a false sense of decorum—teatime and dinner jackets—despite being far from England. He certainly knew the work of Karen Blixen, the Danish author better known as Isak Dinesen, who lived on a coffee plantation in the highlands north of Nairobi. In works like *Out of Africa*, she wrote about the settlers of the early 1900s. Dan was also familiar with the work of a more recent settler, the American artist Peter Beard, who had made collages, photographs, and journals featuring Kenya's native people and endangered animals since the 1960s.

mboru Warriors behind Ngong Hills (right) E

Humph!

MUTHAIGA OPEN
ROTARY PRO
WRESTLING

on is persued by a zebra and horse at Athi

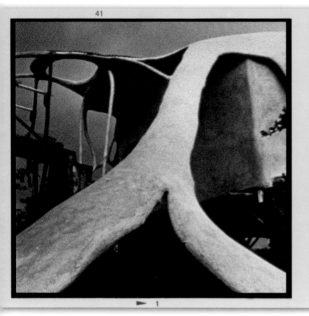

► 1   ►   ► 2   ►

ABOVE: Kitengela, the Crozes' compound, became a second home to Dan.

Dan's first school experience in Kenya was not an altogether good one. Hillcrest Primary School was a traditional British-style private school, complete with uniforms and bristly teachers bent on recitation and good posture.

What made Hillcrest bearable for Dan, other than the drawings he made during classes, was his friendship with Lengai Croze. Lengai first gravitated toward Dan mostly because of his abundant art supplies. During recess, they'd sit together in an enormous old tree at the far end of the playground, making up adventures for the game they'd invented, "Mars Willies." They began by creating a comic storyboard, but the game soon morphed into something requiring guns made of Legos and plenty of running and climbing.

Lengai was the son of an artist and an elephant researcher. When Dan and Lengai first met, the Croze family were living in a double-decker bus north of Nairobi. By 1979, they had bought property in Kitengela, a wild area adjacent to Nairobi National Park, cut through by a deep river gorge. They lived in a tent at first, gradually adding whimsical and rough buildings adorned with the stained-glass windows that Nani, Lengai's mother, made in her studio.

Dan and Amy were global travelers from a young age. Along with Kathy's family, they went to Bermuda and South America. Within Africa, the family spent time in Egypt, Lamu (an island off the coast of Kenya), Ethiopia, and South Africa.

When Dan was about ten years old and Amy was six, the two of them began flying on

Encounter with Hostile
Native Warriors 1985

► 1

their own to Europe and the United States. They'd start their journey in London, staying with their dad's family for a week, then travel on to Iowa to be with Kathy's parents, whom they called Mamo and Umpo, and their large group of cousins. The flight became second nature to them both, though Dan had certain privileges as the older sibling. "He convinced me that it was more comfortable to sleep on the floor," says Amy, "so he always got both seats."

Once in Iowa, they spent several weeks at Camp Wapsie, a YMCA camp that their great-great-grandmother had helped to start and where Kathy had worked as a girl. They returned every year, until Dan was in high school.

We drove to Harvey and Nani's in a borrowed Land Rover, as it has rained and the road was nearly impassable. We arrived late, when the sun was behind the clouds, ringing each one with silver. The animals were all there: the crown crested crane, which always terrifies me, their monkey, assorted ducklings, geese, chickens, the monitor lizard, Egyptian vulture, and the funny little puppy. We ate supper together, sitting in the mud hut dining room and balancing plates on our laps. Then we moved into the sitting room, a vast space under a thatched roof, where we sang Christmas carols and had a traditional German Advent service before being presented with German cookies. We left early as the children had school the next day, but at least we got some Christmas spirit in!

—KATHY, IN A LETTER TO HER MOTHER, 1977

13 people vanish i

fun

They ju
away sa

Vol. 4 — No. 27   July 8, 1986   59¢

Sun

BAG LADY IS

217 TRASHCAN

I remember how very like me he was despite living in Kenya, which to me was a fantastical place that existed only in Tintin books or *National Geographic*. I think he had the same perception. . . . He saw too that other twelve- or thirteen-year-old boys, no matter where they lived, were just like him.

At the same time, living in Africa was a source of great pride for Dan, made obvious in small ways. I still have hand-carved animals he gave me on every visit and a beaded friendship bracelet. I remember him being willing to talk about the culture and animals and other parts of life in Kenya, even though he had just been asked the same questions five times already that day.

—DAVID BRIGHT, WAPSIE CABINMATE

Coupl
cute pu
sell fo

When Dan was ten, he developed stomach pains and headaches that cleared up only when he stayed home from school. It quickly became evident that he was trying to avoid the overly strict atmosphere of Hillcrest, where students were punished by being rapped on the knuckles with a ruler or subjected to tirades. The gym teacher, Mr. Evans, would whack Dan's backside to convince him that morning swims in the school's icy pool were an edifying experience.

Dan's anxiety bouts were frequent enough that he missed weeks of school. Finally, his parents sent him to a doctor whose diagnosis was "school phobia," and the prescription was a transfer to the International School of Kenya (ISK), an American-style school with a more open, creative approach to education. The move separated Dan from his best friend, Lengai, but it banished the aches and pains.

ISK was a new chapter for Dan. It brought an opportunity to be around kids from all over the world. At graduation, he would brag that he'd seen Palestinians and Israelis embrace and that his classmates broke down all stereotypes. The progressive school also gave him more opportunities to travel and explore Kenya through its cultural immersion programs, and it provided a fuller selection of art classes. The school became a second home for him, and he blossomed there.

HIGH SCHOOL

1984–1988

Fifteen was a pivotal year for Dan. That year he first became closely connected with the Maasai people, especially a woman named Kipenget and her family. He was also first exposed to journaling, when his anthropology class took a weeklong trip to a Maasai village with the assignment to keep a detailed journal. Dan began taking his camera with him everywhere, including on impromptu safaris around Nairobi. Over the next four years, he grew from a skinny and somewhat shy kid into a school leader. The pieces that had always been in him—artist, adventurer, and activist—finally connected. Dan became Dan.

Dan was a sophomore when a family friend took him to meet Kipenget, who lived in the Ngong Hills outside Nairobi. The small Maasai woman was mother to half a dozen children. She was married, but her husband was an abusive drunk who appeared only when he needed money. And yet Kipenget, who was illiterate, was always smiling. She saw a kindred spirit in Dan, whom she nicknamed Lesharo, or "the Laughing One."

Kipenget supported her family by making traditional Maasai beaded jewelry. A few times a month, she took a bus to the coastal city of Mombasa to sell her work. Dan started selling her jewelry too, sharing it with family visitors and classmates. For much of his life, he kept stashes of Kipenget's jewelry with him, selling it when he could and returning to her home with money, sugar, and tea.

Dan regularly hitchhiked to Kipenget's small hut about twenty miles north of Nairobi. They would stay up late, telling stories and drinking tea. Eventually Dan would fall asleep in a cowhide hammock along with several of the younger children. In the morning, he and Kipenget's oldest son, Meriape, would take off into the bush, chasing giraffes with Frisbees. Traditionally, young Maasai were supposed to kill a lion, but with big game hunting illegal, new adventures had been invented.

Once, Meriape and his friends inducted Dan in a ceremony meant to mimic the coming-of-age ritual undergone by Maasai boys. Luckily for him, Dan just got to dress up— as opposed to undergoing the usual cultural rite: circumcision.

About the same time that he met Kipenget, Dan went on a weeklong field trip with his high school class to a Maasai village near Mount Kenya. The primary assignment for the trip was to keep a journal. Dan threw himself into it with abandon. He had kept notebooks before, a combination of diary entries and drawings, including one for an English class that same year. But now he was collecting feathers and

eggshells, and rubbing dirt and blood onto the pages.

Dan kept working on the journal until long after it was due. Once he'd finally turned it in, he started his own journal, taking the lessons he'd learned from the anthropology class and applying them to his own art.

ABOVE: Dan and his friend Kipenget look through her jewel

neno: Lalenguyu: one who goes into
laurie's masaipane: the bush and kills
kitts bishop places animals. lacharo.

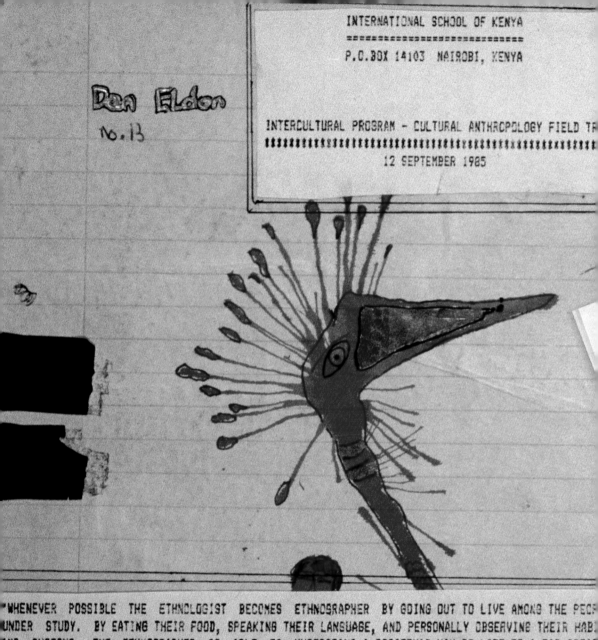

INTERNATIONAL SCHOOL OF KENYA
================================
P.O.BOX 14103 NAIROBI, KENYA

INTERCULTURAL PROGRAM - CULTURAL ANTHROPOLOGY FIELD TR
==
12 SEPTEMBER 1985

"WHENEVER POSSIBLE THE ETHNOLOGIST BECOMES ETHNOGRAPHER BY GOING OUT TO LIVE AMONG THE PEOP
UNDER STUDY. BY EATING THEIR FOOD, SPEAKING THEIR LANGUAGE, AND PERSONALLY OBSERVING THEIR HABI
AND CUSTOMS, THE ETHNOGRAPHER IS ABLE TO UNDERSTAND A SOCIETY'S WAY OF LIFE TO A FAR GREAT
EXTENT THAN ANY "ARMCHAIR ANTHROPOLOGIST" EVER COULD; ONE LEARNS A CULTURE BEST BY LEARNING HOW
BEHAVE ACCEPTABLY ONESELF IN THE SOCIETY IN WHICH ONE IS DOING FIELDWORK. THE ETHNOGRAPHER TRI
TO BECOME A PARTICIPANT-OBSERVER IN THE CULTURE UNDER STUDY. [THIS DOES NOT MEAN THAT MILK MIX
WITH BLOOD HAS TO BE DRUNK IN ORDER TO STUDY THE MAASAI. BUT BY LIVING AMONG MAASAI, T
ETHNOGRAPHER SHOULD BE ABLE TO UNDERSTAND THE ROLE OF THE BLOOD/MILK MIXTURE IN THE OVERA
CULTURAL SCHEME.] HE OR SHE MUST BE A METICULOUS OBSERVER IN ORDER TO BE ABLE TO GET A BRO
OVERVIEW WITHOUT PLACING UNDUE STRESS ON ANY OF ITS COMPONENT PARTS. ONLY BY DISCOVERING HOW
SOCIAL INSTITUTIONS - POLITICAL, ECONOMIC, RELIGIOUS - FIT TOGETHER CAN THE ETHNOGRAPHER BEGIN

Day 5 - the walk

We rose (bright?) and early and started walking up into the hills and through some forest. The temperature was moderate and we went well. The Masai were disgusted by the pase and if we had not held them back, I'm sure that they would have been in Samburu by nightfall! They all took turns carrying the spears but they never stopped looking around. Sali, has Malaria (I think) It looks alot like it what ever it is. Netta fell just as we left but I think that she is all right. When we got into camp 1 goat and one sheep were slaughtered, I helped collect firewood and enlarge the manyatta with thorns and sticks. I found a bushbuck horn and Moses carved a blowing hole in it to make an instrument. We are camped by a fresh water swamp system that is sacred to the Masai.

Being with the Maasai, going down behind the Ngongs as Dan did, well, you can't come back the same person to that sanitized, white world. It makes you very reluctant to return.

— MARY ANNE FITZGERALD, FAMILY FRIEND

MAASAI

Dan grew up with Maasai, seeing them on trips around Kenya's game parks where they lived, or in Nairobi, where many were employed as *askaris*, house guards. He wrote several times about how their ancient seminomadic traditions were being lost to modern, Westernized culture. The Maasai are one of the most recognizable tribes in Africa because of the bright red *shuka*, large swaths of fabric they wear wrapped over one shoulder. They're also known for their walking prowess. Many accounts exist of Maasai appearing seemingly out of nowhere, having walked distances that few other people would undertake. Dan seemed to have emulated them, as few friends could keep up with his long, fast gait.

I could say he'd get wrapped up in it, but it was more than concentration and fascination. Dan would start off with a page or set of pages, build here, write there, ink and blot, or glue materials, then he'd look up and you'd know he'd be thinking, then maybe fidget a little, and get back to building his boat, so to speak. None of this was done in silence—unless he was out of batteries or the electricity went out; he'd do it playing a boom box, mostly reggae, or whatever else he thought was compelling. I have seen him work by candlelight when the electricity went out. He'd just light a candle and get to work . . . like it was calling him, an artistic adrenaline rush.

—LONG WESTERLUND, HIGH SCHOOL FRIEND

From the beginning, Dan's journals were a home for ephemera. He pillaged the house for odds and ends: food labels, cloth, string, ticket stubs, old magazines. When he'd exhausted that supply, he expanded his search zone. The more bizarre or rare the object the better—an Arabic newspaper was more valuable than one in English, the wrapping from a Russian caviar canister better than an everyday soup label.

The journals also became a home for his photographs. Kathy and Mike had given Dan a little automatic camera when he was just six years old. Later, he learned how to use his parents' 35-millimeter cameras and eventually bought his own Nikon from a National Geographic photographer who had stayed at the house for a few days. He often lacked confidence in his abilities as a photographer, which made it all the easier to cut up the photos and draw all over them.

Throughout high school, Dan took more photos of Amy than anyone else. Partly, this reflects how close they were, but it was also a matter of convenience—she was a ready model, willing to have her face painted or to dress up in an odd costume. Her friend Marilyn Kelly was often around and became another of Dan's muses.

RIGHT: Dan decorated the covers of his journals as intensely as he did the inside pages.

Palmistry

cosmos
your hand

The palm's most prominent lines and mounts ("humps" at base of fingers) show dominant character traits. Long lines are most favorable. Each mount is named for a planet and is linked to the planet's influence. Left hand shows traits at birth; right hand, those you have today.

● Head Line ● Heart Line ● Life Line ● Fate Line ● Marriage Lines
☽ Moon, ☿ Mercury, ☉ Sun, ♄ Saturn, ♃ Jupiter, ♀ Venus, ♂ Mars

GRANNY CALLED ATTENTION
TO HER NEW RED WEDGIES.

It started in fifth grade, when Marilyn and I went to a costume party with a Victorian theme and Dan took our pictures. We loved dressing up, and we liked the attention from him. Eventually, he got more involved, positioning us and painting our faces.

—AMY ELDON

LAND ROVER

By the time Dan was in high school, he was one of the rare veterans at the International School of Kenya (ISK). A large number of students, the children of diplomats and business people, stayed in Kenya only a year or two, leading to high turnover at ISK. Dan made it a point to know everyone—from the new kid from Texas to the Asian American with a stutter. He'd stop to talk to the principal, as well as to the groundskeepers, janitors, and cafeteria staff, almost all of whom were black Kenyans and, thus, anonymous to most of the other students.

When he was sixteen, Dan hosted a series of parties to benefit a native Kenyan classmate who needed a heart operation. He turned the cavernous tin building in his family's backyard into a dancehall, calling it *The Mkébe* (or "tin box"), and created decorated invitations that he sold, so that even the people who could not attend were contributing. The parties became legendary in the Nairobi private school set.

After finishing a sociology exam more quickly than the rest of the class, Dan asked to leave the room and was denied permission. He argued with his teacher that, except for the desire to exert control, there was no reason to keep him sitting there. When the teacher still wouldn't budge, Dan bellowed, "You're wasting my youth!" The teacher let him go.

And none of them—from the principal on down—were immune to Dan's salesmanship. A natural flirt and negotiator, he had an innate ability to sell nearly anything. He'd go to a section of downtown Nairobi known as Jua Kali that was filled with little workshops specializing in metalworking, sewing, leather goods, or automotive parts, to name a few. Just about anything could be ordered and manufactured by someone there. Dan's first product was *nunchaku,* a martial arts weapon, which he sold to friends at school. Next, he had boxer shorts sewn in bright patterns.

ABOVE: Workers at Jua Kali.

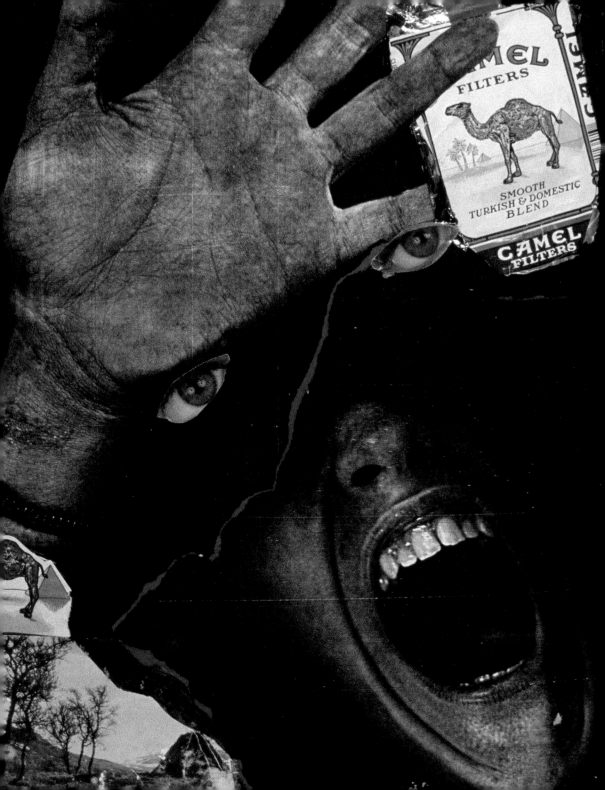

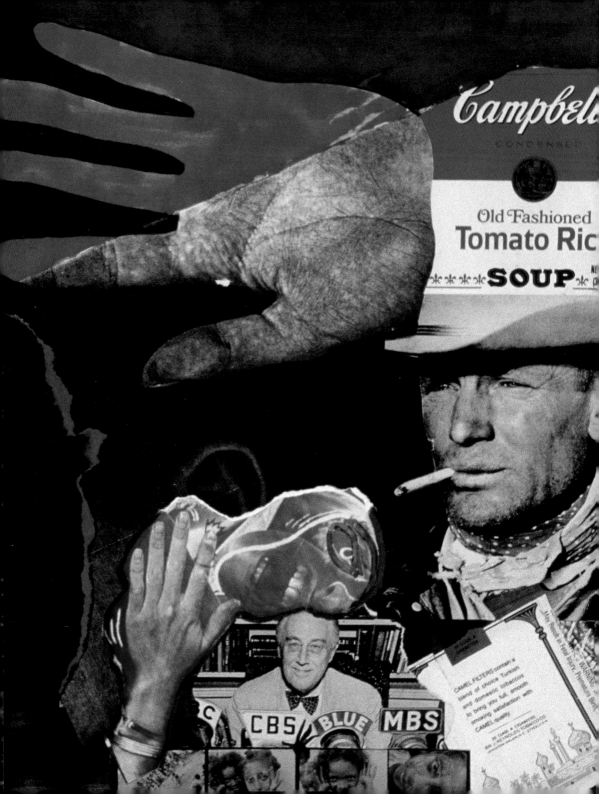

By senior year, Dan was a committed journal keeper who carried his book with him everywhere, as well as his camera and a tin box of art supplies. He'd been known to enlist girlfriends in cutting and pasting rather than go out on a date, and most of his friends were used to hanging out with him in his bedroom, which was really an art studio with a bed.

He worked on several journals at once, revisiting earlier pages and making changes. As a result, the journals aren't chronological. Dan often created series of images—some taken from his own photographs, others borrowed from famous works, such as a portrait of jazz trumpeter Miles Davis—that he'd rework using different techniques.

One of his favorite parts of senior year was the International Baccalaureate art class that he took with several good friends. They spent the year experimenting with various mediums and styles. *The Shock of the New*, a famous introduction to modern art, was their primary textbook, and its spirit of boundarypushing served as inspiration. In printmaking, they tried to make the most authentic dollar bills possible. Then, in photography, they cut up photos to mimic the work of David Hockney and tried every chemical combination they could in the darkroom.

Dan didn't think much of his own drawings. When he tried to do a realistic portrait of someone, he struggled with the proportions. What his drawings lacked in specificity, however, they made up for in vivaciousness and humor. He loved cartooning and could cleverly skewer a topic.

DEDAN KIMATHI

Dan often took the same image and re-worked it in multiple styles using different mediums. This was the approach he took to one of his heroes, Dedan Kimathi, often using a photo of him lying on a stretcher. Kimathi was the leader of the Mau Mau, a group considered freedom fighters by some and terrorists by others, who led an uprising against the British colonialists during the 1950s. He lived in the forest around Mount Kenya and became a mythic figure for his ability to avoid capture by the British. Eventually, however, he was caught and hung. In 2007, a statue would be erected in downtown Nairobi to pay homage to his role in helping Kenya gain independence.

FIELD MARSHAL DEDAN KIMATHI WACIURI

Dan spent considerable time exploring Nairobi, going to parts of town that whites, especially white teenagers, rarely visited. He loved taking *matatus,* which Dan called "the Kenyan subway." People pack themselves in, with some hanging off the sides. Dan had favorite haunts—an Indian restaurant on River Road, a sandwich shop that sold croissants. He loved playing with the street kids who sold toys they made out of recycled wires and aluminum scraps. He'd put on a great show of trying to decide which toy airplane or car to buy before paying the chosen child. In the back of his car was a large collection of other toys and knickknacks he'd bought on the street.

Dan sometimes took *matatus* to the coast near Mombasa or up north to Maralal. On one such trip, he met a Samburu *moran* (young warrior) about his age, Enkroine. Like the Maasai, the Samburu warriors were known for their physical prowess and self-confidence that bordered on arrogance. The two struck up a friendship and spent time together at Enkroine's village. Dan once wrote a school paper about Enkroine.

One morning we had to catch a bus at five. We had no alarm clock (obviously), so Enkroine's solution was to stay awake all night under the influence of *miraa*. He also has a secret passion for Orbit chewing gum, which fills his mouth when it is void of twigs.

—DAN, FROM A SCHOOL PAPER

Patā Potea, patā potea, pata potea, pata potea!

Patā Potea, Patā Potea

In Africa, this rhythm is more common than any drumbeat ever was.

I AM WALKIN through thi at a ranch Northern K

Translated from Kiswahili, "Patā Potea" means... "Find one, lose one" and is the nickname given to flipflops Because of the noise they make.

Patu Potea Patu Potea

I tried to make the de others. I failed so he wa a stone gripped in his mou why they called him 'Obelix' He is the father of pupp

Flipflops Vanish are just as frequently as socks that traditionally 'eaten' by the washing machine in Western culture. I have lost many pairs of flipflops, Maybe two pairs for each of my ten years in Kenya.

WHERE DO THEY GO?

For the most part, people take them. Sometimes borrowed and never returned but usually stolen.

When at the coast, many are abducted and make their way to India by high tide

They devour bushes thi Obelix does not. H waving his tail lik They ignore him

After years of being hunted there is man and where there is ma lifting a demolition ball they raise their They inhale the 'bouquet' of the bush

Their hoofs hammer into climax. I have lost a flip flop and sound like this "Patu, patu, Patu." I eject the other as it only hinders me. Now the Sound is crunching. My bare feet Absorb thorns like a hoover.

I veer up the incline of the hill and thrash straight through a wait-a-bit bush. It's fishook thorns shred my shirt and decorate my skin with intricate patterns of scratches and blood. I risk turning. The bulls are no where in sight. Obelix has appeared beside me. I pry the stone from his mouth and clunk him on the head with it. I am still in danger and my body knows it. I feel sight, sound and smell like a lifelong veil has been lifted from my senses. Because of this, I feel great. Pato Potea, my heart beats, enriched with adrenelin. Every tree is a possible escape ladder, in every wind change the fear of betrayal. My destination lies at the end of this labyrinth of bush guarded by now invisible minotours.

Obelix senses my feelings and grabs a stone. I boot him in the head. Together we approach the house and I begin to feel the pain in my feet and corregated back like a tightrope of barbed wire.

2 BUFFALO. I HATE BUFFALO. Even walking past the stuffed buffalo in the museum makes me cringe I'm glad I saw these old bulls first. Noiselessly, I back off away. ...ces after them and barkin... ...k for me. ...know that where there is dog, ...is a gun. Like a crane ...e heads and peer around. ...conisseur checking for impurities.

...k up from Obelix ...'d see

I hobble into the kitchen and the Samburu cooks stare at me. "Buffalo," I gasp, lurching for the sink. As I wash my feet, one of them asks "Where are your shoes?" "Out there." I tell them I lost them one cook is already gone. Later that night, I hear him walking to his hut...

Pato Potea, Patu Potea,

at home with the ...long next to me with ...ways does this, thats cartoon character ...he trains to ...de rocks too.

In the spring of his senior year, Dan visited his friend Roberta on her ranch north of Nairobi, along with several friends and his girlfriend. With its sparse beauty, the ranch was one of Dan's favorite places. While his friends lounged by the pool, Dan went for a walk, joined by his friend's dog, Obelix. They ended up having a close encounter with a water buffalo. Dan would remember it as a near-death experience, and the water buffalo came to symbolize ultimate evil for him.

It wasn't surprising that at the end of senior year Dan was chosen to speak at graduation. Nor was it unexpected that he found a unique way to address his ISK experience. He borrowed a term from the novelist Kurt Vonnegut: *karass.*

Leaving ISK turned out to be hard on Dan. He had been a big fish in a small but delightful pond. In New York the next fall, he would suffer from a depression that he hadn't known since his Hillcrest days, a loneliness that would occasionally haunt him. It was his own dark buffalo.

ABOVE: The Eldons at Dan's graduation from ISK.

LA MANO

I have recently read a book by Kurt Vonnegut in which he describes a group of people such as a class, religion, or even a country as being Granfalloons. These are groups of people joined together by a common characteristic or by chance but not necessarily by choice. . . . When people are together because of friendship or love alone, Vonnegut calls their relationship a "Karass." . . .

At ISK, thanks to the outstanding Intercultural program, many of us have had opportunities to meet people from all parts of Kenya and often find Karass members in a remote village or island. . . .

The school has given us the chance to venture north to Turkana with the vast desert and the Samburu tribe. We can travel east to Lamu, with mosques, dhows and the Swahili people. We have gone west to visit the people of Lake Victoria in their homes and schools. We even go up, to the top of Mount Kenya with rugged mountain guides and a case or two of frostbite. On these trips, it is always interesting to see which aspects of culture rub off on whom. It is just as funny seeing a boy who has lived his whole life in Ohio gulping down a sufiria of blood with the Maasai as it is seeing the Warrior standing next to him brandishing a spear and an ISK baseball cap.

We leave much behind tonight: hard wooden chairs, asking permission to go to the rest room, raising hands before speaking. But I hope that we can bring with us our friends, our Karass.

Finally, I ask the parents and teachers here tonight, Were your high school days "some of the best in your life," like I have heard so many times? If it is so, I hope it will not be the case for us. School days are fun, but I'm looking forward to things getting better and better for us until our last days. Because our fiftieth class reunion is going to be at the Mkebe, and it's going to be wild.

-DAN ELDON, GRADUATION SPEECH

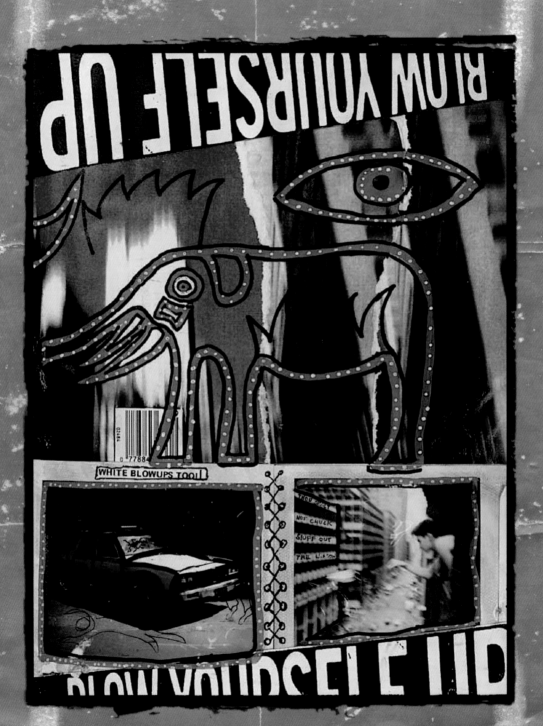

"Live, on Safari!"

THE YEAR "ON"

Fall 1988–1989

During his senior year at ISK, most of Dan's friends were waiting to hear about acceptances from Oxford, Cambridge, Yale, and the like. Dan hadn't done particularly well on his SATs, largely due to dyslexia, so he was not expecting any such letter. Instead, he was eager to gain more practical experiences.

He told his guidance counselor that he was trying to get an internship at an American magazine and was also hoping to travel through southern Africa after graduation. "So, you're taking a year off?" the counselor asked.

"No," Dan said, "I'm taking the year on."

The year "on" started with a three-month internship at *Mademoiselle*, a New York–based fashion magazine. Dan had visited their offices the previous summer after one of the Eldons' houseguests had arranged for him to take a tour. He'd shown the art staff his current journal, and they were so taken with it that they made T-shirts from the images, going so far as to run to a corner market to buy the plain shirts while he toured the rest of the office. When Dan returned, they were all wearing a different one of his images.

It didn't take long for Dan to charm the magazine's all-female art staff. The office was very communal, without walls or individual offices. This was before magazines were designed on computers; instead, layouts were done by hand. Dan did a bit of everything, from running errands and making photocopies to planning several layouts that ended up in print. Once, for a piece about graffiti-influenced fashion, the editors gave him a pair of black high-tops to decorate with a silver marker, and the sneakers ended up in the shoot.

He spent a lot of time playing with the office's top-of-the-line color photocopier, reproducing journal pages in multiple colors and sizes. His journal from this time shows a new design savvy as he increasingly created full-page spreads that were tighter in their overall concept and layout.

We were all in awe of the journals. I think each of us wanted to run off to Africa after hearing his stories.

—KATI KORPIJAAKKO,
ART DIRECTOR, *MADEMOISELLE*

KATHY AND DELPHI

One night before he'd graduated from high school, Kathy came into Dan's room and sat with him while he worked on a journal. She'd recently returned from a trip to Greece and had decided, after many months of tortured indecision, to leave her husband and move to London. Dan was guarded about her decision, not wanting to talk.

"I sat down next to him, took up a pen, and asked him to draw his emotions," Kathy remembers. He reached for a thick black Magic Marker and drew a bleeding antelope caught in a barbed wire fence, its anguished face reflecting bewilderment, fear, and pain. He added the words "Distrust" and "Betrayal" to the margin.

"Now you draw, Mum," he said, holding out a pen. Kathy drew a woman taking flight. She told him about visiting Delphi in Greece, with its ancient inscription: "Know thyself." Dan wouldn't look at her. "It's what I'm trying to do," Kathy insisted.

Finally, Dan looked up. "It's okay, Mum. I understand what you are doing. I am proud of you. It takes courage to do what you're doing. Don't worry; we'll be okay."

Thinking about New York and how many radio waves are going out—music, police cars, taxis, planes. We must absorb and feel the waves. That could explain the feeling one gets when in New York compared to being in Kenya.

—DAN, FROM A JOURNAL

Dan often paired images of Africa and New York, a commentary on two very different kinds of wildness. The sky became an obsession as he longed for the big open spaces of Africa. He approached New York as he did Nairobi—a grand adventure, taking safaris to lesser-known and poorer neighborhoods. He talked with cabbies, street vendors, and the homeless. One night in Penn Station, he was mugged at knifepoint. Dropping his metal art box as a distraction, Dan quickly pulled a twenty from his wallet, threw it at the mugger, and took off running.

As creatively fertile as the city was for him, it was also emotionally isolating. New York made him claustrophobic. He was painfully aware that his family was separated, with Kathy in London, him in the States, and Mike and Amy back in Kenya. Without the safety of home and school, he fell into the old depression that had occasionally dogged him. By Christmas, he was ready to go back to Africa.

I approached Dr. Croze in London and suggested that we meet in the city to discuss what I called a "matter of some interest". Dr. Croze was free from academic responsibility because the silly bastard had just been booted out of school for climbing on the roof.

We agreed to meet at Pizza Hut and it was there that I proposed the idea of an expedition penetrating deep into the African bush. Dr. Croze was immediately receptive to the idea of another pizza Americano but was hesitant to respond to my proposition. "Good Lord, Eldon, do you know what you're suggesting? Are you serious." he queried.

"My dear boy" I responded, "I have never been more serious in my entire life." Croze sensed the urgency in my tone of voice... the time was right. I withdrew the map of Africa from my tunic and clapped it down on the pizza in front of Dr. Croze. He slowly inserted the monicle into his eye and unfolded the enormous map onto the table and onto the table of the six skin-headed gentlemen adjacent to ourselves. "Oi, watch yourself bogey face" they quipped as they stabbed a fork into the head of Dr. Croze. Dr. Croze, being a serious academic and a man of the church, was unused to such strong language and after smashing up the young hooligans we sat back down. Crozes face grew pink with glee as his pale, watery, onion coloured eyes traced the route that my long, elegant, aristocratic fingers pointed to. In fact it was after looking at the waitress that we got back to the map.

The plan was to drive my recently purchased Land Rover from Nairobi to as far south as humanly possible in a clapped out old Land Rover that was, in fact the same Land Rover that Napoleon used in the Battle of Midway Island in 1066.

We shook hands and Croze earnestly pledged that no matter what happened, I would pick up the bill for the pizzas.

We then proceeded to the bank where Dr. Croze grappled with the automatic cash machine. You must understand that Dr. Croze is very much an old world gentleman and unused to such modern affairs.

All we had to do now was to convince Lengai's dad to shell out the cash that would make the epic voyage possible.

ABOVE: Dan on a picnic with Saskia.
OPPOSITE: Dan with ISK friends, taking
Dezirée on a maiden safari.

Arriving back in Kenya after Christmas, Dan purchased an old Land Rover. The rusted truck came with two beds, a camper top, a gas grill and small refrigerator, and jerry cans for water. Dan had convinced his grandfather to pay for part of Dezirée—as he named her arguing that she provided a key to learning through adventure during his year "on." Not entirely convinced, his grandfather was nonetheless impressed by Dan's power of persuasion.

Dezirée became another canvas, an extension of the journals. Dan tricked her out with a cow's skull mounted above the front window. He glued Mexican playing cards, fortunes, newspaper clippings, and postcards to the inside ceiling and painted the steering wheel with the words "Fight the Power."

He and a group of friends, including a girl-friend named Saskia, tried Dez out on a series of mini safaris, trekking up to the Kenyan highlands and out to the ocean.

By August, Dan and Lengai had a plan for a much bigger safari. They would drive as far south as Dezirée would take them—to Lake Malawi, or better yet, to Victoria Falls.

Princess
Knows £370
AU

great punch...
Deziree. Tex
descended the
hills while
all beat each
up and tried t
throw Pierre of
the moving veh

The Kikuyu
Princess
herself at "shady
hadquaters...
Carnivore

"White Cap"

Deziree

459

e tries to save Deziree from tipping over
er we got over ambitious on climbing the
gong hills.

TEAM
Deziree
an

The Deziree
crew rest after
exhausting picnic
and some rou
wine pro
by Pierre.
Photo by
Peter M
the day
after his
operation.

Note
angle

O 459

TO 159

he tries to train hi

tes feet and faced Tex to
(of honey wine beer)

ROAD
MOMBASA

LAND
ROVER

At some point, Lengai would have to leave to start college in England, and Dan would continue on his own.

Convincing their parents was the first challenge. Malaria, political strife, and bandits were just some of the concerns. Dan emphasized what a great learning experience it would all be. They enlisted another friend, Patrick Falconer, who had plans to go to medical school, as their chief medic, and at last their parents relented.

⊗⊗⊗

August 10, 1989
After much debate the previous night, we woke at 0500 hours and completed the final packing. Tex and Pierre arrived later to offer a few words of no confidence. After a formal farewell ceremony, Dezirée roars to life and we shred down the driveway and onto the open road. We return a few minutes later for the cold box.

⊗⊗⊗

One of the challenges of the trip was getting through border crossings. Every time they passed from one country into another, they had to negotiate forms, payments, and corruption on both sides of the border. Entering Tanzania, they were forced to give up all the beer from their cooler to guards who wanted it for themselves.

They picked up hitchhikers, navigated bathtub-size potholes, and stopped frequently to repair Dezirée. Once, at four A.M., while Lengai and Patrick slept, Dan was driving when the gearshift came off in his hands. "What part of the car is this?" he hollered, waking Lengai and shaking the gearshift in his face. Lengai and Patrick managed to manipulate the gears into the right position using a long screwdriver, which they then used as a gearshift until they could find a welder the next day.

Along the way, they removed the driver's front door to improve ventilation and welded iron bars over the back window space after a thief broke the pane. When the starter broke, they had to resort to hand cranking Dezirée to life.

The first stop was Lake Malawi, where they played with kids and flirted with girls.

From there, they went to Blantyre, the biggest city in Malawi, where they were able to take their first hot showers of the trip and eat some decent food.

KENYA LAND ROVER

Deziree

LONDON 1989

CROZE, A. LENGAI, DR.

Leningrad, 1902
P.h.d. Minsk University
Explosives expert,
Karate black-belt,
High Altitude Skydiver,
Baboon dentist.

ELDON, DANIEL ROBERT

Algeria, 1958
Ex-Mafia hit man,
Ex-Sub-Aquatic Accountant,
Legion Etrangés C.I.A.
and also, a very nice
bloke.

August 20, 1989
Monkey Bay
Find Blantyre's sports club by accident. Chill out with Euros at bar. Have excellent showers. Eat pepper steak—highlight of trip. Start on whiskey and beer—don't stop. Chat up girls. Lengai makes fool out of himself through chatting and repetition. Lengai loses stomach, sleeps in bushes with shoes on.

A few days later, Patrick flew home. Lengai would have to go soon as well, but first they were determined to see Victoria Falls—one of the Seven Wonders of the Natural World. Getting to Zimbabwe meant crossing Mozambique's so-called Gun Run. Once a week, a wide dusty path, the only route across the war-torn country, was cleared of landmines. A convoy of about two hundred cars and trucks met to cross together on those days—safety in numbers.

Halfway through the chaotic hundred-mile road race, everyone stopped to refuel and regain their nerves, before taking off again. It was in Tete, the midway point, that Dan and Lengai first glimpsed Mozambicans who had been living under warfare for more than a decade. It was a much different face of Africa than Dan had previously encountered.

After so many years of civil war, this sun-baked town on the Zambezi River is in a very sad state. There is very little in the shops, with even bread, milk, rice, and sodas unavailable. The only cars around are clapped-out heaps that would be in a scrap yard in most other countries. Marxist slogans are crudely stenciled in Portuguese on the crumbling walls. They denounce capitalism and praise the glory that the people's revolution has brought to their country.

Dan and Lengai camped in Harare, the capital of Zimbabwe, for a few days. The urban sprawl was markedly different from the rest of the trip, as they slept in parking lots and ate at fast-food chains.

August 25, 1989
Dr. Croze and myself arrived in Harare late Tuesday night and sought asylum at the Holiday Inn. We docked the U.S.S. Desirée outside the aforementioned establishment and camped in what was admittedly the most urban location we had habitated to date. Gone were the cries of distant hyenas and lions; instead, the colorful language of street people could be heard,

bargaining for female flesh, and the magical clattering of some bastard trying to pull the shovel off the back of the car.

We both knew that the time had come to play mini golf—we made our way to the Mini Put-Put and did a quick twelve holes. This was not what we had driven across Africa for, so we went to the water slides and chatted up the "cleavage sisters," two young ladies with much more bust than racial understanding. In fact, they were racist bitches. But you must understand that Dr. Croze and myself had been living in very harsh bush conditions and a quiet desperation had settled in.

❀❀❀

The next day, they left Dezirée at the airport and flew to Victoria Falls, where they spent two days exploring, crashing hotel swimming pools, and chasing a group of nuns whom Dan was intent on photographing.

❀❀❀

August 26, 1989
Dr. Croze and I have reached a place on the Zambezi River where this great body of water plummets 100m into rocks below—the result is not altogether unspectacular.

❀❀❀

After visiting the falls, Lengai departed for school in England, and Dan spent another week in Harare. He met a girl named Nancy Todd, and her family took him in for the week. One night, Dan accompanied Mr. Todd to a dance. As night fell, the dancers encircled Dan in a ceremony that was a combination of ancient rite and surreal apocalyptic dance party.

September 4, 1989

Go back to dance. I sit on car and am surrounded by sixty kids. They ask me to dance. I give it like crazy. They form a circle. They sing, drum, and cheer. They sing for me; then I sing for them. I shake one of their hands, then I almost swim across their mass of hands as they touch and grab me in a nice way. They Jit Jive again, then Berti calls me over and we drink beer.

Berti tells me to hold on because they are going to give me an African name. And it could be frightening. I see them gather up stones. I am led to the center of crowd and thrown to the ground. Lights shine on me. Dust, moon, and fire—drums reach frenzy. Devil dancer comes out and beckons me. Lunges at me. Kisses me by rubbing mask against my face. The old man is holding me down and the woman is screaming in front of me. He pulls three young girls from the crowd and they Jit Jive around my face. I am pulled up, given three coins, and named Auraga Chikawait Chata *after the three dancers. It means* He Who Kills the One Who Messes Around with His Wife. *The crowd cries out my name.*

❦

For the next three weeks, Dan hitchhiked around South Africa. His goal was to get by on five dollars a day. If a driver didn't take him in for the night, then he'd go to the local police station and check himself into a cell. The police found it amusing but never turned him away.

As he traveled, talking to both the whites and the blacks, he tried to learn about apartheid firsthand. He never recorded his reaction but provided snapshots of the level of pure racism that was openly expressed in South Africa at that time.

❦

Truck stops three miles down road. Young white guy: "People say we're racist down here, but not true." The truth is they're animals. They killed seven people last week, and they expect the world to treat them like human beings.

❦

Dan happened to be in Cape Town on September 13 and attended a historically significant march. He'd slept in a youth hostel the night before, where he'd heard rumors about a protest forming at a church. Camera in hand, he spent the day trying to find the highest vantage point from which to shoot. He tried

77

Apartheid, which means "separate" in Afrikaans, was a legalized system of separating racial groups following the end of South Africa's colonial rule in 1948. The government recognized four groups: whites, blacks, "coloreds" (people of mixed race), and Indians. Although whites were by far the minority in the country, they controlled the government and the business sector. As a result, they had a much higher standard of living in all areas, including housing, schooling, and even length of life. Blacks lived in ghettos where their homes were made of tin roofs, cardboard, and mud.

Strong opposition arose in the 1950s, and early leaders in this movement, including Nelson Mandela, who later became the first black president of South Africa, were imprisoned. Groups of people continued to organize, including young people who marched in the streets of Soweto in 1976 to protest the fact that they had to pay to attend school. As many as six hundred were killed in the Soweto uprising.

By the late 1980s, apartheid was under attack from abroad, as economic sanctions by other nations and major corporations were destabilizing the economy. More South Africans supported the opposition, and protests were increasingly mixed race, with many whites participating. On September 13, 1989, several weeks following a protest that had turned violent, there was a large march from Parliament to St. George's Cathedral, led by Desmond Tutu, a black South African cleric who had already won the Nobel Peace Prize. Thirty thousand people of all ages and races showed up in a tremendous display of nonviolent unity. Dan was there.

Township residents demonstrate defiance during funeral. Alexandria, 1986

Noel Watson

to get press credentials—something he would have known about from working with his mom on newspaper articles in Kenya—but wasn't successful. Nonetheless, the event was his first real introduction to how photojournalists cover political upheaval.

❦❦❦

September 13, 1989
Got some samosas and a Coke and proceed to church where I had observed something going down. A crowd had assembled bearing placards, which read antiapartheid slogans. There was much chanting of Amanda Wetu and singing about Oliver Tambo, Nelson Mandela. . . . Climb on cars to get better view—told to get down. Journalists up in trees, telling people to turn banners around. Hundreds of students, old people, fat mamas, young guys marching, dancing, good spirits. . . . Tutu makes crowd join hands. Calls for de Klerk to listen to the peaceful people. Holds up hands—shows they are empty. "He will be the last white South African P.M."

❦❦❦

After the protest, Dan spent another week in South Africa before returning to Harare to pick up Dezirée. She'd been repaired and was ready to head back to Lake Malawi, where Dan's dad met him for a few days of camping and swimming. Dan then lazily retraced his route, finally arriving in Nairobi in mid-October. The year "on" was essentially over. Next stop: California.

ar Mum,
ere is a tape
your listening
asure. It includes
e music to cheer
up, like the
ath scene from
ita and some
lgarian Funeral music
m not joking!)
ell, it sounds like
real party over
ere! I am happy to
announce
that
things
over
here

excellent! (that is,
you happen to like rice

my classes are interesting
and I am really
excited about the Photo class!

I am going to
try and look for a
job for tuesdays
and thursdays. I have
met a nice girl
(Mexican)
well
how
goes!
and
see
it
It sounds like Amy
is doing quite well
for herself.

Thats devotion,
writing 'I love
mum' on grains
of rice, But
what is she
thinking? why is
he writing on rice
and not reading
French Assignments.
You can't win.

The main point is, that
I love you very much
even if you are
low on energy or
blood.
I am sad that
you feel sick and
I think about how
you are at least
every twenty minutes
lots of
love,
Dan.

さけ祭づけ

RICE LOVE Mum I LOVE I LOVE Mum

FEB.
1990
CALIFORNIA
USA

Laurie has had
her little heart
broken. But sends
her love to you
all.

 દૂરદર્શન
મંગળવાર, તા. ૨૪-૧-'૮૯
ચેનલ - ૧.
સાંજે : ૫-૪૫, લોકસંગીત, ૬-૦૦
જ્ઞાનદીપ, ૬-૩૦ અપના ઉત્સવ સમાપન
સમારોહનું જીવંત પ્રસારણ, ૭-૩૦ મરાઠીમાં
સમાચાર, ૭-૪૫ સપ્રેમ નમસ્કાર, ૮-૦૦
સામાજિક સુરક્ષિતતા યોજના, ૮-૧૦ ચાલ
નાવાચી વાચાળ વસ્તી : મરાઠીમાં પ્રાયોજિત
કાર્યક્રમ, રાષ્ટ્રીય કાર્યક્રમ ૮-૪૦ હિન્દીમાં
સમાચાર, ૯-૦૦ જીવન રેખા, ૯-૩૦
અંગ્રેજીમાં સમાચાર, ૯-૫૦ કિલ્લે કા રહસ્ય,
૧૦-૨૦ ૧૨મા ઈન્ટરનેશનલ ફિલ્મ ફેસ્ટીવલ
ઑફ ઈન્ડીયા નો સમાપન સમારોહ - ટી.વી.
અહેવાલ. ૧૦-૫૦ ડૉન બોસ્કો - અ ફ્રેન્ડ
ઑફ ૫ યંગ - ચૂત્રચિત્ર, ૧૧-૧૫ સમાપ્ત.
બીજ ચેનલ

NDEZ
ERS
Diet
Coke
DONT
WALK
TACO
BELL
AND NEW GIRL
ND
IN
T

THINKING
GOOD
THOUGHTS
TO
YOU.
X.
V
VI

In my mind, I still am planning
another Adventure... the Desert, the great area... void of culture or life.
Freezing at times but burning hot at others. No this is not Iowa,
I'm talking about its the Sahara!

Fig a.

92°

105

Yea, the rumors are [...]
eople in malawi do [...]
ats and they enjoy [...]
t. We felt it releasa [...]
t purchase some for [...]
efves and some of our [...]
embers sampled the [...]
knows locally

MKEBE MKEBE MKEBE MKEBE MKEBE

MKEBE MKEBE MKEBE MKEBE MKEB

Mandrake

Croze, A.L.

STA

STUDENT TRANSPORT AID

January–September 1990

In January 1990, Dan arrived in Southern California to begin classes at Pasadena Community College. Though he was in Los Angeles physically, his heart and mind were still very much in Africa. The refugees he'd met from the civil war in Mozambique were especially on his mind. Their plight had shown him a side of Africa he'd never seen before, and he was sure that something could and should be done to help them. At the very least, he could use his entrepreneurial skills to raise money.

One of the first people Dan met when he arrived was Eiji Shimizu, a Japanese exchange student. They decided to find a place together. One night, while watching a documentary about Africa, Dan told Eiji about the refugees in Malawi. Together, they made a pact to do something about it. Within weeks, the two had come up with Student Transport Aid (STA), to raise money for the refugees, and began recruiting friends to join them. But it soon became obvious that simply donating the money wasn't nearly enough. They were determined to go to Malawi themselves.

What began as a simple fund-raising effort soon turned into an adventure of a lifetime for the members of STA, who came from six different countries. Ultimately they hand-delivered thousands of dollars directly to one of Africa's largest refugee camps, and it changed them all forever.

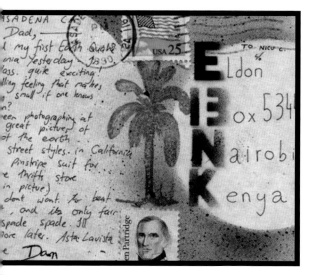

Dan and Eiji's apartment served as STA headquarters. They put a big jar by the front door to collect spare change from any and all visitors. "Empty your pockets upon entering," was the refrain. Team members met there regularly to plan and share meals, practicing what Dan called "sincere cooking." This often meant rice and beans but cooked with the best of intentions.

They enlisted other friends to the cause, including Akiko Tomioka, another Japanese exchange student, whom Dan was dating, and Twumasi Weisel, an old ISK friend who was also attending school in Los Angeles. Twumasi was living with family friends and brought on board their two college-aged kids, Hayden and Ryan Bixby. At twenty-one years old, Hayden was STA's eldest member.

Fund-raising began by staffing a table on the campus commons where they handed out flyers about the war in Mozambique. Dan clandestinely made T-shirts in the school's art studio, which they sold along with Kipenget's bracelets. They visited local charitable organizations and made presentations in hopes of gaining sponsorship.

I've been dating several girls—a Filipino, a Latina, and a Japanese. I like the Japanese one the best. Her name is Akiko, and she's always smiling.

—DAN, 1990

Dear Marte!
How is it?!
Thank you for
your wild post card I love hearing from
you. It makes me feel good for ten hours.

KJEKKEN Ø SAFARIS

April 10 1990

USA—

I like California alot, but my mind is still
in Africa. Since I got back from Africa, I have
been working on a project to raise money for
Mozambique. This summer, a group of friends will
drive down through Kenya, Tanzania and Malawi,
to visit the refugees on the border. I want
you to come. If you come, we need you
to write in Norwegen articles for papers there.
We hope to make a video and I will take
photos of the situation there.

The trip will be July 1st → Aug 20 and
will probably be big big fun. On the way down, It
will be the best across Africa party since Livingstone!
Write to me NOW. If you can come you will need
to get a round trip ticket to Kenya, АЭРОФЛОТ
and about $1000 for the trip.

Ask the other Norwegens, Danes and Swedes if they
want to come too, it
will be the wickedest
and wildest event eve.

AFRICA 1990
KENYA TANZANIA MALAWI ZAMBIA

OTHER OLD FRIENDS
DAN TEX MARIE AMY

THE CROC. THAT ATE MURDOCH

As their fund-raising efforts grew, so did the plans. They decided that they couldn't trust an aid group to determine where the money ended up. Instead, they needed to go to the refugee camp themselves to see what was most needed.

With a big trip now in the works, the team expanded. Amy, living in London at the time, got involved, recruiting her high school's student council to donate all of the money from the soda machine to STA. Robert Gobright, an old ISK classmate, and Lengai signed on as the team mechanics. A friend of Lengai's from boarding school, Chris Nolan, agreed to help film the adventure. Dan wrote to an old ISK flame, Marte Rambourg, and she got a job at a 7-Eleven in Oslo to earn money for the trip. Others came on at the last minute, and some had to bow out, mainly because their parents felt that a group of young people traveling across eastern Africa in a Land Rover was not the safest plan for summer vacation. By the time June rolled around, fourteen STA members from ages sixteen to twenty-one and with six native languages between them had officially signed on. They had raised nearly twenty thousand dollars.

ROKO BELIC
Age: 18
Hometown: Chicago 'burbs

When Roko was growing up, his mother removed the knob from the TV so that it was frozen on PBS; the nature shows he watched there ultimately inspired his love of travel. When he heard about STA, Roko drove to Los Angeles from his college in Santa Barbara, was hugely taken with Dan and his journals, and signed up.

AMY ELDON
Age: turned 16 on the trip
Hometown: Nairobi

Little sister Amy kept Dan steady when things got tense. Although she was already well-traveled in Africa, years later she said that seeing her home continent through the eyes of the other travelers helped her to understand and appreciate it in a new way.

HAYDEN BIXBY
Age: 21
Hometown: Los Angeles

Hayden had already been to Kenya as a study-abroad student, where she'd fallen in love with the country. Hayden was close to both Eiji and Dan and, as the oldest member of the team, sometimes provided them counsel.

LENGAI CROZE
Age: 19
Hometown: the bush around Nairobi

Aka "Legs" or "Dr. Croze," Dan's best friend, Lengai had the touch to keep Deziree running. Much to Dan's consternation, he also had a soft spot for Marte.

RYAN BIXBY
Age: 19
Hometown: Los Angeles

Hayden's younger brother, Ryan became so dedicated to raising money for STA that he dropped a class during spring semester.

JEFFREY GETTLEMAN
Age: 19
Hometown: Chicago 'burbs

Jeff was in college at Cornell University when his best friend from high school, Roko Belic, recruited him for STA.

DAN ELDON
Age: 19
Hometown: Nairobi

Chief instigator, organizer, and chronicler.

1990 Kenya - Malawi ✗✗✗✗✗✗✗✗

CHRISTOPHER NOLAN
Age: 19
Hometown: Chicago 'burbs

Chris met Lengai during a year at a British boarding school and had visited him in Kenya the year before. Chris and Roko, who had been making films together since childhood, agreed to film the trip.

LORRAINE GOVINDEN
Age: 17
Hometown: Los Angeles

Lorraine, aka "Chaka Chaka," got involved with STA because she was dating Ryan. Once in Africa, she challenged the team's patience with imagined fevers, a very public coughing fit, and a lost passport.

MARTE RAMBORG
Age: 18
Hometown: Oslo

A former ISK student, Marte was already in love with Africa. Having spent one very romantic night with Dan, including sunset on Mt. Kenya with a Maasai family, she was eager to return.

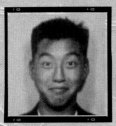

EIJI SHIMIZU
Age: 19
Hometown: Tokyo

Chief accountant, Eiji, or "A.J. Hans," was in charge of all cash on the trip.

ELINOR TATUM
Age: 18
Hometown: Manhattan

Eli found out about STA via a family friend. Although she didn't meet Dan and the others until she arrived in Nairobi, she was one of the group's top fund-raisers, heavily working her family's Upper East Side network. On the trip, Eli was the chief crepe maker.

AKIKO TOMIOKA
Age: 18
Hometown: Tokyo

A student at Pasadena Community College, Akiko and Dan dated during the STA planning phase. Dan affectionately called her "Squid Girl," a name that stuck on the trip.

ROBERT GOBRIGHT
Age: 18
Hometown: Seattle

Robert and Dan knew each other from ISK. Robert was one of the main mechanics on the trip and also the team grump. He was wary of those who hadn't been to Africa before, believing they wouldn't pull their weight.

free at last...

الدكتور يربن زيلدن

ABOVE: Eli, Akiko, and Marte study a map in the front seat of Dezirée.

Team members began arriving in Nairobi around mid-June and all gathered at Mike Eldon's house. Several members of the group had never been in Africa before and had plenty of culture shock to deal with. Roko Belic and Jeff Gettleman, Chris Nolan's friends from Chicago, had barely been in Nairobi when they found themselves in the midst of a large political riot. They managed to outrun the violence, which killed several people, though they were plenty rattled.

The first order of business was to find a second vehicle. Dan and Lengai bought a used Toyota from a man who was leaving Nairobi, and they christened it Arabella, after the song "Mentirosa" by Mellow Man Ace. Outfitting the trip with food and supplies came next.

By July 10, they were finally ready to leave Kenya. It would take three weeks to travel to Mwanza, one of the largest refugee camps in Malawi. Driving in two vehicles, the fourteen STA members and their supplies were literally jammed in. Two people sat in the front seat of each truck, three in the backseat, and another two sprawled in the far back and bouncing around with the cargo. Because of the intense dust caused by the unpaved roads, the drivers often wore bandanas over their mouths. Dan wired a boom box to Dezirée's dashboard, which blasted reggae and African ska as they jolted along.

At night, the group camped out inside the trucks, on top of them, and on the ground. Once, they illegally spent the night in a national park and had to sneak out at dawn. A few times, they stayed in seedy motels with spring-popped mattresses, sleeping two or even three to a bed. They were lucky to find a running shower and luckier still to be able to purchase a hamburger or tepid Coke at a restaurant. Mainly, they subsisted on mangoes, crepes cooked by team member Eli Tatum, runny yogurt, and canned beans.

The illegal campsite in Mikumi National Park. The next morning, we busted out through a newly made road. Made, in fact, by Dr. Croze and I

...living the dramatic

Each person reacted differently to the stress of extreme travel. Eli cooked. Rob huffed when woken up too early. Amy and Marte spent time applying more makeup than seemed necessary given the circumstances. Hayden stuck her nose in a book and retreated. Roko and Jeff tried to be helpful but rarely were; Dan called them the Shoulder Pat Boys for their American habit of placing their hands on people's shoulders in what was meant as a reassuring gesture. Ryan was distracted by taking care of his girlfriend, Lorraine, who seemed to be sick much of the time.

Border crossings were especially unnerving. Dan and Lengai would collect everyone's passports and try to deal as calmly as possible with the guards, who usually demanded bribes. Once, they tricked Jeff and Roko into believing that they would have to cut off their long hair in order to enter a country.

Other, more minor crises seemed to pop up daily. With fourteen people crammed into two hot, dusty trucks, poor sleeping arrangements, and unfamiliar food, it was only a matter of time before people got cranky. Little riffs between team members became the norm, and everyone turned to Dan for help, no matter how large or small the problem. Finally, when it seemed the group was at a breaking point, Dan stepped up and suggested an art project—decorating Dezirée and Arabella. While everyone came together for once, Dan simply passed out art supplies and quietly watched from the side.

ABOVE: The Number 18 spanner—or wrench—was reserved for team members in need of an attitude adjustment.

BA S m sa

dan
marte
lengai

"The bad Samosa" 1990

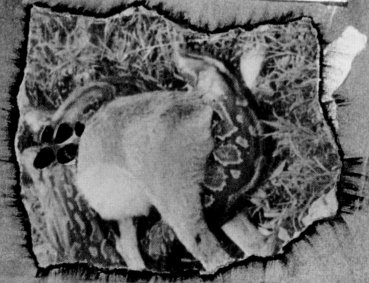

"The protruding nail will be hammered into place" Japanese Maxim.

"The Evil That Mzungus do"

THE STRUGGLE CONTINUES

J. is the victim of a ritual watermelon sacrifice

Most distracting of all, however, was the love triangle that had developed among Dan, Lengai, and Marte. Though Dan had dated Akiko all spring, he hoped that romance might be rekindled with Marte. He was unhappy that she'd been flirting with Lengai, and the tension between the three of them boiled throughout Tanzania. When, finally, it was clear her full attention was on Lengai, Dan's mood turned black.

He pouted and moped and created a dark journal page that he showed to Hayden before gluing it together. Finally, Amy told him to snap out of it. "The team needs you," she counseled. The next morning he was back to his old self and stuck a new bumper sticker on Dezirée that read "Positive Vibrations."

Just as with the trip the previous summer, Lake Malawi was a beautiful and relaxing reprieve. The team camped on the beach for several nights, enjoyed good food, and befriended a group of British teenagers who were also camping there (with chaperones). A brave few tasted the local roadside specialty— roasted rat.

Dear Mum,

It is Sept. 18th and I am twenty years old. Well, its been quite a life so far and I want to say thank you for all the energy and input that you gave! For things like getting me the camera and making me excited about making things and building things and drawing things and writing things. I think that these are some of the things that I enjoy most about my mission on earth.

We just set up the dark room that you thought of getting all those years ago, and we are producing some good results already.

The safari went very well, as you obviously have heard already. I'll have to say that I learned alot some of it fun and some was almost a night-mare.

I'll have to be careful, because when the trouble started on the trip, I emotionally started a down-spiral that reminded me of those bad times when I was young. I didn't think that that side of me was still around, but it is in there somewhere.

I have almost finished a new journal - I have to start a new one for the big safari. I hear you are doing some good stuff on the bath room wall etc.

Dad is very happy but very busy with the 10th ann. exhibition. He has tons of women after him as usual.

You sound very well and doing interesting jobs. I love you very much and I'm sorry I did not write enough. Lots of Love, Dan..

A.J. and I went to the Red Cross and had the displeasure of meeting Marcel, the director, who told us how insignificant the contribution would be for such a large organization like theirs. Arabella then proceeded to stall and refused to start in the driveway.

—DAN, 1990

REFUGEE MURAL

rom Mozambique . . .

MOZAMBIQUE

Although the STA team never entered Mozambique, they skirted the border. After weeks of a road-trip vibe, the group suddenly became serious. The area was a wasteland without trees or bushes and desolation was the presiding mood. Mozambique had known nothing but war for nearly three decades. First had come the war for independence against Portugal, followed swiftly by a civil war between government forces (FRELIMO) and guerrillas (RENAMO) who were backed by South Africa and Rhodesia.

In the decade-long civil war, nearly a million people died, many from starvation after farms and medical facilities were purposely destroyed. Almost half of the country's schools were also leveled. Not that anyone could go to school: five and a half million people were displaced with a million of those seeking refuge in neighboring countries. Two enormous problems that haunted the country and slowed rebuilding for years after the war were the use of mutilation by guerrilla forces, who disabled many people when they burned their hands and ears for being "uncooperative," and land mines. An estimated two million land mines were planted in Mozambique during both wars.

When peace was finally declared in 1992 and multiparty elections were first held, the United Nations gave Mozambique the ignominious title of the world's poorest nation.

PAULINA FATIMA		DOMINGOS JOSE		FLORA RAFAEL ZECA		ADAO USSENE/QUERINO		QUISITO MARCOS	
FEM.	6 ANOS	MASC.	8 ANOS	FEM.	9 ANOS	MASC.	11 ANOS	MASC.	13 ANOS
		JOSE		RAFAEL ZECA		USSENE		MARCOS DOMINGOS	
FATIMA		NORA		ANA HENRIQUE		ROSALINA		LUISA BELEZA	
MUTARARA VILA NOVA		MUTARARA VILA NOVA		MUTARARA VILA NOVA		MUTARARA VILA NOVA		CHARRE	
MUTARARA		MUTARARA		MUTARARA		MUTARARA		MUTARARA	
TETE		TETE		TETE		TETE		TETE	

MIGUEL TENENTE		PAULINA SAIZE/LINA		MARQUES ALBANO		JOSE THENESSE/JOSINHO		LEONOR LUIS/MARIZANE	
MASC.	11 ANOS	FEM.	12 ANOS	MASC.	15 ANOS	MASC.	16 ANOS	FEM.	13 ANOS
TENENTE		SAIZE THOLE NOTA		ALBANO JESSENAO		THENESSE IANGAKWAO		LUIS CHICO	
ELISA ARMANDO		ANA GEMUSSE		FATIMA KVENGVE		NSTSAE ALFER		DOMINGAS ANTONIO	
CHARRE		INHANGOMA		MUTARARA VILA NOVA		MUTARARA SEDE		MUTARARA VILA NOVA	
MUTARARA		MUTARARA		MUTARARA		MUTARARA		MUTARARA	
TETE		TETE		TETE		TETE		TETE	

The team arrived at Mwanza Camp, located near Blantyre, Malawi, on July 31 and slept there for several nights while they interviewed aid groups, toured the camp, and learned about the refugees' day-to-day lives. They were surprised by how well organized the camp was. It had been started by the United Nations and nongovernmental organizations, such as Save the Children, that created schools and a medical clinic, provided materials for housing, and distributed food. The refugees seemed relatively happy, especially the children who roared with laughter whenever Dan put on his gorilla mask. Many of the kids had been born there and knew no other home.

The camp held plenty of unsettling reminders of war, too, including bulletin boards covered with photos of missing family members, many of them children, and people baring scars and disfigurements. The refugees had come up with creative ways of remembering what their home had been like, as well as recalling the injuries of war. They made music, told stories, and painted murals around the camp. One night, Hayden and Chris followed a group of people into the woods for a dance. They watched as the adults pantomimed specific movements. Then, as they were invited to join in, they realized that the dance was a reenactment of the war.

Every evening, the STA members met up to report back what they'd learned during the day and to discuss ideas for how their money might be spent. (The cash had been stuffed into pillows and closely monitored by Eiji, the team accountant, who dispensed necessary amounts for repairs, border crossings, and the like.) After several team meetings, they voted and decided that clean drinking water was the most essential need, so they gave the bulk of the funds to the Norwegian Refugee Council to build wells for drinking water. The wells were ultimately named Dezirée and Arabella. The remainder went to purchase blankets for a medical clinic. They gave Arabella to another group, along with some money for her upkeep as she was on her last legs.

Once the money had been donated, the group quickly dispersed, with some members heading home immediately, others tacking on travel around Africa, and Dan and a small cadre driving Dezirée back to Nairobi. Each of them left with a sense of accomplishment, as well as with sureness that they would all be together again. For years, Dan talked about organizing a second STA trip, but it never came together.

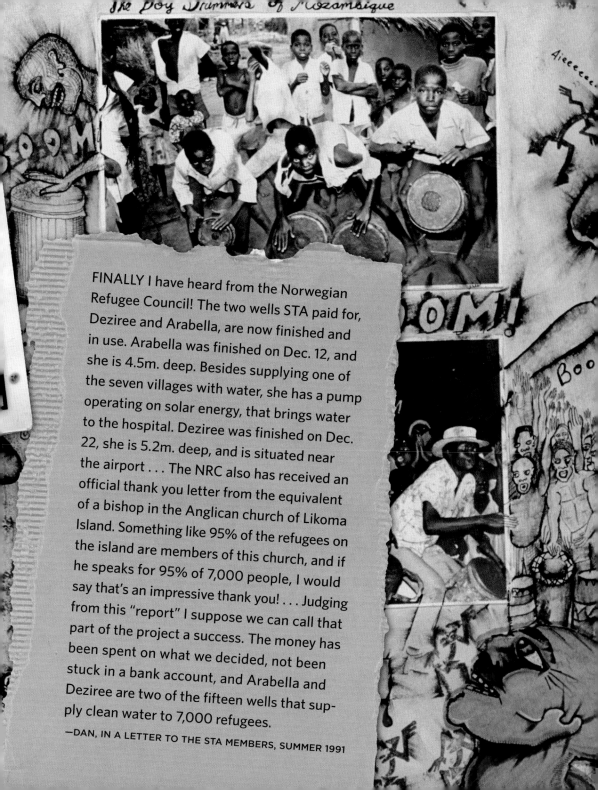

The Boy Drummers of Mozambique

FINALLY I have heard from the Norwegian Refugee Council! The two wells STA paid for, Deziree and Arabella, are now finished and in use. Arabella was finished on Dec. 12, and she is 4.5m. deep. Besides supplying one of the seven villages with water, she has a pump operating on solar energy, that brings water to the hospital. Deziree was finished on Dec. 22, she is 5.2m. deep, and is situated near the airport . . . The NRC also has received an official thank you letter from the equivalent of a bishop in the Anglican church of Likoma Island. Something like 95% of the refugees on the island are members of this church, and if he speaks for 95% of 7,000 people, I would say that's an impressive thank you! . . . Judging from this "report" I suppose we can call that part of the project a success. The money has been spent on what we decided, not been stuck in a bank account, and Arabella and Deziree are two of the fifteen wells that supply clean water to 7,000 refugees.

—DAN, IN A LETTER TO THE STA MEMBERS, SUMMER 1991

...am Deziree Africa Exploration
...n Eldon
...x 53441
...robi
...nya
... 254-2-750131

The "Oasis Deziree" and "Wadi el Arabella" built 1990

DEZIREE
DONATED BY
...RY TRANSPORT...

ARABELLA
DONATED BY
...ELLDON TRANSPORT LTD

out of
100

le in

a is
rugee.

are

rillion
se in

ia.

"Our voyage to bring fresh potable, clear drinking water for the village in the
camp. To provide an oasis with which the refugees can drink and
irrigate their crops. We named the wells "Arabella and Desiree"
We also donated a Land Cruiser to assist with the transportation of
agricultural aid for small scale garden plots that allow families to

A funny thing happens to one who is traveling and does not look in the mirror for days.

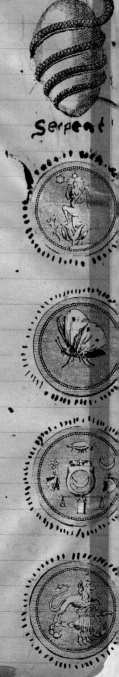

Serpent

LIFE ● ON SAFARI

October 1990–June 1992

The year "on" was based on Dan's principal motto: "Safari as a way of life." For Westerners, a *safari* is a trip involving big game hunting, or in today's world of ecotourism, a trip into the bush to see and photograph animals. But the word, which is Swahili by origin, has a much broader meaning: *departure, expedition,* and *journey* are its closest synonyms.

Dan used safaris as a way to encounter himself and others. While in LA, he roused friends from the TV to go on a "safari" in the seediest part of South Central, ending at a biker bar that appeared menacing but from which Dan emerged with bear hugs and invitations to come back the next day. In Nairobi, he dressed up as a priest and went to a hotel to hide in plain sight from friends who were having lunch there. A safari could take him across town, out into the dark night of the countryside, or to a different part of the world by way of a rickety airplane on the cheapest ticket possible.

Spiritual seekers are often reminded to live in the moment. That's what travel did for Dan: It grounded him in the Now. He took several grand safaris in his life—the trip south with Lengai and the STA journey—but there were many shorter safaris as well, each seemingly more quixotic than the last, many of them occurring during the two years between STA and when he eventually took a job as a photojournalist.

Dan's safaris began in high school, first hitchhiking out to Kipenget's and then taking up-country *matatus* to Maralal. Geographically, Maralal is about two hours northwest of Kenya, but it has the spirit of a rough-and-tumble frontier town. It was the place to which Dan retreated when he needed to detox from life, so it made sense that he'd go there shortly after returning from STA—its arid desolation was an antidote to the chaos of that trip. He took only a video camera and a notebook with him.

Northern Kenya Oct. 28, 1990
Frontier town.
Everyone is armed; things are sharp.

O.k. I finally have a lot to say, but I don't want to write the usual self-centered white man traveling in Africa story. I'm sick of films and books set in third world places about Euros floating around and showing the scene through their eyes. But I am a white man cruising around Africa, so I'm going to give you the usual self-centered crap.

My first thought has nothing to do with anything but not many of my thoughts do right now. When you have been driving for twenty-four hours straight and have not looked into a mirror for weeks except for your own dusty reflection on the speedometer glass, you run out of things to think about. So you start to think about new things.

I like things made of canvas, metal, wood, and steel, like Deziree. I'm sick of plastic. I don't want to start talking like some old man, but I like quality. The only good thing about living in

up North. Sit by t

Waiting for cold soda at the Pop In hotel in Mar

the olden days before the 1950s was that things really were made nicely. But again, I'm not saying that I want to go back in time or anything because people used to be sadistic animals. Old people always get off on how these days young people are dangerous rapists, drug addicts, and gangsters, which is true, but think about all the stuff they got up to. Only for them, they had it organized by the government. I mean think about it. What's worse? The gang situation in Los Angeles or World War II?

I had a discussion with my grandmother about it. She tries to tell me that these days things are uncivilized and dangerous, but I told her that back in her times, things were worse, like making black people sit in the back of the bus and using different toilets. Imagine? Now is the best time to live. Anyway, I was talking about quality. I got my hands on an FN self-loading assault rifle at one of the police checks today and fondled it extensively. I love things that click and slide into place and are well oiled. The most seductive

sound in the world is a well-greased rifle cocking into position.

I've only had guns pointed at me a few times, but it always feels good—the ultimate test of "what do I say now." The final examination for the manipulator. Manipulation. Negative word, yes? But I think it's got a bad name because many bad people are good at it. The concept itself is fine as long as the person uses it wisely.

. . . I've got the video hooked up to the car battery, go into villages, record the people there and then show them themselves in black-and-white moving around inside a tiny box. Reminds me of something I read about a European filmmaker who took a load of film of some guys in a remote part of Ethiopia and then came back the next year and showed them the film. Unfortunately, one of the characters in the film had died during the year and then they see him moving around in the white man's box. Try explaining that.

indow and watch this cowli
African Rednecks   town

The Place is run by Somalis and is my h

Girlfriends were often the impetus for Dan's safaris. Late in the fall of 1990, he went to Tokyo, largely out of a desire to see Akiko. He got a month-long job teaching English and stayed at a friend's apartment. Akiko was different than she'd been in Africa—more self-conscious and less carefree. She also had a boyfriend. Dan didn't particularly care for Japan either. He was overwhelmed by the crowds and turned off by the rules and obsession with cleanliness. "I really feel like James T. Kirk on *Star Trek* on a weirdo planet," he wrote to a friend.

In January 1991, Dan moved to London to attend college. He lived on campus at Richmond University, bonding with his French roommate and seeking out any Africans he could find. He fought with his photography professor, who gave him a B-minus for not following assignments. Mostly, though, he spent time hanging out with Amy and exploring London with his camera.

In the spring, he persuaded his grandmother Gaby to help him buy a Land Rover. She was as unsure about this plan as his maternal grandfather had been, but Mike came to Dan's rescue, reassuring his mother that her grandson would get something educationally sound out of the experiences the truck would bring him. Dan named the rig Big Blue and took to driving it around the British countryside on weekends. His grand scheme was to drive to Morocco via Spain and buy leather goods and jewelry. He'd then ship Big Blue to the United States and outfit her as a mobile shop, driving around to college campuses to sell his African wares and using the proceeds to fund a second STA trip.

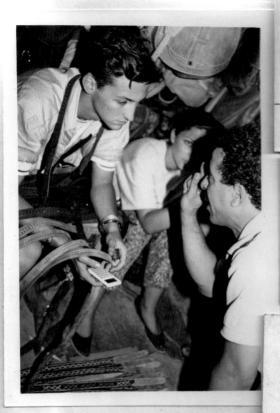

He persuaded Amy and Lengai to make the trip south with him—sort of an STA Lite. After meandering through Spain, they visited the souks of Tangiers and Fez. These giant outdoor markets are so large that entire city blocks are given over to just a single craft or product, such as carpets. On the outer ring, snake charmers and kids with trained monkeys provide entertainment, while stalls heaped with date nuts and squeezed-to-order orange juice keep shoppers fed. Farther back in the labyrinth, over cups of sweetened mint tea, customers and merchants barter over carpets and leather goods.

The three friends spent days checking out the merchandise and bartering with silver and leather-good merchants. They bought heaps of necklaces and belts, which turned out to smell intensely of dung. Once they got to Casablanca, they packed it all up so that Amy and Lengai could transport their haul to London. Dan planned to buy more before finding a ship to take him and Big Blue to New York. But before his friend and sister even left, the Land Rover broke down. The next few weeks were a dull, hot waiting game. Dan bought a scooter to get around town. Every day, he visited the mechanic. Every day, he took more pictures. He went a little crazy, which ended up being a good thing for his journals. He produced dozens of entries based on his time in Morocco, and they are among his best.

I rode through the slums and was mobbed by thirty children who pelted me with stones and stuck branches in the spokes of my tires. Later in the day, two teenage gang members grabbed me by my throat and only released me when I produced a canister of tear gas and waved it in their general direction. Today, I was approached by a young troublemaker who was interested in my camera. I again went for the CS gas but in my haste to free it, I discharged it onto my leg while it was still in my pocket. The assailant must have taken pity on the solitary European *étranger*, because when I had stopped writhing in agony, he was nowhere to be seen.

—DAN, FROM A NOTEBOOK KEPT WHILE IN MOROCCO

When Big Blue was finally fixed, Dan had lost too much time to take a ship. He had to be in California to start the fall school semester. Instead, he drove Big Blue back to London, parked her outside his mother's apartment, and headed to the United States by plane.

"Her name is Dezirée" he smiles lovingly.

when I looked into the bright round eyes I was totally absorbed.

The room seemed to fade away into blackness – all I could see was two balls of light. Then I realized... this is what the blind man sees. The eyes more inten...

Those eyes were burning hotter and brighter b...

then in a violent sudden explosion they shattered like

a. The grand "Bazar". Roasting of brochettes.

b. Casablanca Zabu market

There were things in [the]
I had never seen, creatures
that I never knew

were passing
perfumes and
[fragrance?] of every
[descr]iption. The smell [of] death
thick in the [air?]
There was no [magic?] in my
mind... If there was [such a?]
thing as magic,

Dan's reentry to the United States found him in a much different place than on previous visits. He wasn't the lonely, recent high school graduate he'd been in New York; nor was his time consumed by STA planning, as it had been during his previous stint in LA. Now, he was taking extension classes at UCLA with the hopes of eventually getting into the university's famed film program. He somehow talked his way into a penthouse apartment in the Kappa Sigma fraternity on campus. As Eiji—who was living in LA that fall, too, recalls, "How the hell this outsider to the fraternity convinced the brothers to let him use the best property is still beyond me."

When he wasn't taking classes at UCLA, Dan was often on Venice Beach selling the belts and trinkets he'd bought in Morocco. His mother had schlepped several boxes from London to Los Angeles for him. Viewing it as an opportunity for theatrics, he'd wear a World War I aviator helmet and try out various accents. He liked it when people haggled with him, African style. When a cop threatened to give him a ticket for selling without a license, he tried to strike a bargain, suggesting the man's wife would enjoy a necklace. He won.

Over Thanksgiving break, unable to get back to Iowa to be with his family, and in search of an adventure, Dan went on a short safari to Mexico. He used the experience as material for an English paper when he returned.

RIGHT: Dan attended some of the fraternity parties that fall. When a large fight broke out one night, he grabbed his camera, climbed up high, and covered the action just as he would a riot in Africa.

Los Angeles Police

Testing for drunk drivers over the Holiday season

HOLLYWOOD TATTOO
6317 HOLLYWOOD BLVD.
HOLLYWOOD, CA
(213) 464-9938

TATTOO ARTIST
JAY AND **JOANNA**

ONE OF THE FINEST TATTOO STUDIO
EXPERTS IN ALL STYLES, DETAILED WORK,
CUSTOM DESIGNS, COVER-UPS
STERILIZED EQUIPMENT

OPEN AT 1 PM DAILY

QUICK SMOG & BRAKES
COMPLETE AUTO SERVICE

"get out of the car, sir."

—I think we got one here

Los Angeles Police at Topanga Canyon

 partment

The great thing about the United States is that you can go anywhere in the world not far from your house. Last weekend was the Thai New Year. I went to the park and saw the whole scene with dancers, monks, etc. I was the only *mzungu* there except for some sleazy fellows who had mail-order Thai brides. On May 5, the Mexicans had their party, and I went to Santa Monica beach and, again, I was the only *mzungu*.

—DAN, IN A POSTCARD TO HIS DAD

Scandal!

What is superman doing
outside the adult
theatre with three young
Mexican children?

Hollywood 1991

Thanksgiving, 1991

Before the Thanksgiving break, I tried to explain to my Japanese friend why I was sad. Everyone in the house was leaving or had left for happy family weekends at home, and my only relative in California is a third cousin from Romania who was cremated seven years ago. My friend suggested that I should go to Las Vegas, proving the fact that Thanksgiving is really not an integral part of the Japanese family calendar. I told him that that would be like listening to a Walkman in his ancestor's shrine or spending Christmas in a brothel, but I don't think that he really understood. Instead of Las Vegas, I decided to drive down to Mexico.

There were strong winds on the freeway and my little brown Ford Tempo with Iowa plates felt more like a rowboat on the open sea as I battled to keep her on course southwards down the mighty "Interstate 5." I began to imagine myself as Papillon, escaping from a Los Angeles that sometimes feels like a nightmarish penal colony. When I reached the border, the image was complete: the massive gates and walls of fortress America. Border Patrol guards, wearing cowboy hats and bandolier belts bristling with clubs, cuffs, stun guns, mace, and pistols scanned no-man's-land with enormous green telescopes to see through darkness.

The strange thing about the American Fortress border is that it is designed to keep people out. As I crossed into Mexico, I saw the faces of thousands of people who would do almost anything to get into America. America is such an exclusive club, and my first Thanksgiving lesson was that I am damned lucky to have pictures of me glued into two little blue books; one with an embossed golden eagle holding some arrows and the other with the rampant lion and unicorn of Her Majesty's government.

I am so lucky to have been born in the right place at the right time with the right parents. My life is so easy without even having to struggle for it. . . .

My weekend in Mexico was fantastic. Two days of gluttony. . . . I drove back to Los Angeles on Sunday night with a surfer I met. He was actually Persian, and his family had decided to leave Iran after the Shah died. His father had worked for the Ministry of Finance so it seemed to him that it would be a good time to move the family to the United States and it would help if they took along with them a good part of the National

Treasury. I dropped him off at his girlfriend's house and then slept for the rest of Monday. At around 7:00 P.M. the surfer's girlfriend called me on the phone with an emergency. One of the dozen oysters that he had eaten in Mexico must have been bad and he needed to go to the hospital. There were two more problems: The girlfriend had no car, and the surfer had no insurance. For someone who does not believe in fate, this double coincidence is almost too dismal to fathom. The chances of meeting someone in America with no form of motorized transportation and no medical coverage are astronomical.

I climbed into the brown Ford again and followed the now infamous Interstate 5 to pick him up. We called every hospital, but all of them wanted huge amounts of money to repair my Persian's innards. I started a halfhearted argument with the UCLA medical emergency receptionist about the Hippocratic oath and basic human decency. The LA County Hospital in East Los Angeles is the only institution apparently that has ever heard of such an oath and that is where we arrived at 10:45 at night. I have grown up in Africa and am used to seeing rundown hospitals, but LA County looks like a cross between M*A*S*H and the Battle of the Somme. I checked the patient in at the desk and picked him up six and a half hours later. During those hours I was taught my final Thanksgiving lessons.

I stood in the waiting room against the wall and braced myself for the horror. Every ten minutes a snarling, manacled convict would be led through, drenched in blood or crusty with vomit. Old Latina women wept in groups as children wandered around looking bewildered. Half of the people in the room were just homeless who came in with their shopping bags and rags and shower caps to watch TV and escape the cold. Everyone there was miles below the poverty level and here we were trying to get an oyster out of a Persian surfer.

I decided to make a collect call to my grandmother in Iowa to pass the time. She asked me if I was eating well and if I had heard about Magic Johnson and that us young people should be very careful these days. While I talked, the sheriff's department dragged three gang members past, screaming in Spanish. My grandma asked what all the noise was and how I was enjoying Los

Homeless in Berkeley 199

For Dan, as for me, the greatest joy was in taking pictures of people. Not furtive distant shots taken in the hope that "the subject" wouldn't notice they'd been snapped. No, a joyful encounter that resulted in them posing willingly as part of the building of a relationship. It shows in the pictures, and it remains in the memory as a respectful, dignified encounter.

—MIKE ELDON

I am on the airplane now.
Virgin, London to L.A.

I want to do great
things in my life - I want
the plane to land, so I
can start. The only
problem is where do I start.
What do I do when I
get off the plane to
do great things?

Is University the best
place for me. Should
I take off with my camera
to El Salvador. Listen to
what your heart tells you,
you say. Well I'd like to
rip the little bastard out
and interrogate him with a
12 volt car battery.

CREATIVITY + ENERGY

Angeles. I said the fraternity where I was living was a bit noisy, but I was enjoying my classes and I got an A- on my African history midterm. She said that they all missed me in Iowa for Thanksgiving and everyone sent lots of love and a big hug.

⊗⊗⊗

Dan flew back to Nairobi for winter break with the intent of spending a few weeks connecting with old friends and his dad, then flying through London to see his mother before returning to LA for a second semester. Instead, he ended up in four extremely different countries in the course of a few weeks and ultimately landed in Iowa—not California.

During the first few weeks of break, his attention was completely captured by Soiya Gecaga, one of Amy's best friends. The grand-daughter of Kenya's first president, Jomo Kenyatta, Soiya was Kenyan royalty,

accustomed to high-end travel, expensive clothing, and bodyguards. Dan enjoyed teasing her and trying to get her out of her prim and proper ways. Soiya, on the other hand, was determined not to become one of Dan's many conquests. He complained to her that her "head kept overly strict exit visas" and he hadn't "even gotten near her first border town."

Around Christmas, Mike, Amy, and Dan traveled to India, where Mike and Dan had a great time playing dueling photographers, with Amy as their occasional muse. Dan had gotten his penchant for photography from his dad, and though his eye was now strong enough to outstrip his father's—not unlike a kid who plays tennis with a parent for years and suddenly, one day, can beat him—the two always loved going out in a new landscape with cameras in hand.

Dan and Lengai were perfecting the short, cheap trip. Over Easter, they'd gone to Berlin, taking a train and staying with distant relatives. When Dan reached London, they purchased the least expensive tickets they could find for a forty-eight-hour trip and ended up on a wobbly Aeroflot flight to Moscow, Dan wearing no more than a thin jacket.

Days later, he was on a plane for Los Angeles. Soon after arriving, he changed his plans and took off for Iowa. He spent the winter living with his cousin and taking classes at a local college. His mother offered him a job on a film project but wasn't sure when it would start. Uncertain of what he wanted to do next, Dan tried to remain flexible. Other ideas—trips, schooling, work—were brewing in his head, too. He wrote Soiya from the plane, wondering what he should do next:

I want to do great things in my life. I want the plane to land, so I can start. The only problem is where do I start? What do I do when I get off the plane to do great things? Is university the best place for me? Should I take off with my camera to El Salvador? Listen to what your heart tells you, you say. Well I'd like to rip the little bastard out and interrogate him with a twelve-volt car battery.

❦❦❦

By early spring, his mother called and said the film was starting in Kenya. It was time to come home.

Dan's job as third assistant director on Kathy's film, *Lost in Africa*, turned out to be no more than that of a glorified gofer. But Dan was in his element. For two months, he was up at dawn to copy call sheets and distribute them

BELOW: Dan and Kathy on the set of *Lost in Africa*.

Well, well, well. Mt. Vernon, Iowa. The places that I end up. Quite a flight path: Nairobi, Moscow, London, Los Angeles, Mt. Vernon, Iowa. What would the CIA make of me? The town here is quiet. Very quiet. The natives are mainly involved in small-scale agriculture, the trading of swine and sweet potatoes and such. I have found them friendly and quite harmless. The climate is not entirely unarctic, if you will excuse the double negative. I am acclimating to the conditions and am able to remain outdoors for fifteen to twenty seconds now.

—DAN, IN A POSTCARD TO MIKE

A FAMILY OF TRAVELERS

Dan's passports held stamps from more than forty different countries. His wanderlust can be traced back to his maternal grandparents, Russell and Louise Knapp. Their 1932 honeymoon was only a two-hour car trip and then a jaunt back to a tiny and sparse apartment. But by 1960, they were doing well enough to take their kids on a grand tour of Europe, visiting fourteen countries, attending the summer Olympics in Rome, and spending several days in Moscow, where their phone was tapped in the pre-glasnost era. In the coming decades, the entire family traveled the globe, together and separately, but none outdid Russ and Louise, who saw nearly seventy countries, including China, Zambia, Burma, and the remote Inca ruins of Machu Picchu in Peru.

ABOVE: Louise, John, Janet, Russell, and Kathy Knapp in Moscow.

under the cast and crew's hotel doors. The rest of the day was a mad dash of odd and odder jobs. He quieted people on the set, delivered coffee, parked cars, and held a parasol for a finicky British actor. Once in the late afternoon, the director decided that camels were needed for the morning shoot. The task of finding some was given to Dan, who spent the evening on a scavenger hunt. When he finally located seven of the notoriously temperamental animals, he slept with them in the bush near the set so they wouldn't run away.

安全
SAFETY MATCHE
中國製造 MADE IN CHINA

left: Neema
fresh and
clean from the
shower in
Em's house
July '92

Belau, Roberto's ...

Borrowing a camera from one of the crew-members, Dan began making his own film, *Leila*, about a young Somali woman who moves from the north of Kenya to the city. It starred his new girlfriend, Neema, and his childhood friend Marilyn Kelly.

The film turned out to be amateurish at best, but Dan and Neema's relationship continued to develop well after it was completed. A beautiful young woman used to being the center of attention, Neema was often distant with Dan. When he arrived to take her out, she'd sometimes keep him waiting for hours while she changed clothes and talked to her girl-friends. At clubs, she openly flirted with other men. Dan never knew if it was a ruse to make him more intrigued in her. If it was, it worked— Dan was hooked like never before. He was no closer, however, to knowing what to do next with his twelve-volt heart.

SOMALIA

Becoming a photojournalist who covered wars was not an improbable jump for Dan. Plenty of photographers, some of them war correspondents, had sat around the Eldon family dinner table over the years. Dan grew up hanging out in the offices of the Kenyan newspaper the *Nation* and tagging along with his mom, who wrote restaurant reviews and style articles for them. Just a few years earlier, while hitchhiking in South Africa, he'd watched photographers at work covering the huge antiapartheid rallies. And on two different trips to Mozambique, he'd witnessed the effects of one of the continent's longest civil wars.

Dan was a traveler. An artist. And an African. Becoming a photojournalist brought all of these together. The fact that his photography might ultimately help others by exposing a massive and yet largely overlooked tragedy only made the work more urgent to him. Hundreds of people were dying every day in Somalia, and yet it wasn't registering in the international media. Could a young, unpublished, and self-taught photographer make a difference? Dan was willing to find out.

Dan had done freelance photography for several Nairobi magazines for a number of years, but in the spring of 1992 he started freelancing for the *Nation*, too. A young staff reporter, Aidan Hartley, took an interest in Dan and invited him for lunch one day. Dan showed him some photos he'd recently taken of a male circumcision ceremony, and Aidan was impressed. When Aidan asked what Dan was going to do next, he offered half a dozen unsure possibilities. Aidan told him that it seemed like a no-brainer: For anyone who wanted to be a journalistic photographer, Africa was the place to be. Many of the biggest names in the business were working nearby or would be coming soon. Civil wars and famine seemed to be moving through East Africa like dominoes. In particular, two of Kenya's neighbors, Sudan and Somalia, were in the midst of stark upheaval.

"You can go back to Los Angeles and deconstruct *The Godfather* in film class for the millionth time, or you could stay in your own backyard and do real work," Aidan challenged him. Within a three-hour flight from Nairobi, one could be in the midst of five or six different war zones. Now, that was reality.

"Somalia and Sudan have moved into our guest bedroom" Dan had written to his dad from Iowa just a few months earlier. He knew there were refugees streaming into northern Kenya as a result of the two brewing civil wars. Even before talking with Aidan, he had headed

Me and my clan against the world; me and my family against my clan; me and my brother against my family; me against my brother.

—SOMALI PROVERB

up to Wajir, a town in northern Kenya with one of the largest refugee camps. What he saw there only hinted at the enormity of what must be occurring in Somalia.

Before they'd finished talking, Dan had decided. "When can we go?" he asked Aidan, and in just a few days they were on a plane heading to Mogadishu.

On July 5, 1992, Dan and Aidan flew into "Mog" on a twin-prop plane carrying UNICEF personnel. Mogadishu had once been a beautiful seaside city with pastel stucco mansions, excellent seafood restaurants, and palm-tree-lined streets. Now it was decimated. For two years, warring militias had fought each other from street to street with AK-47s, rocket launchers, and grenades. The few standing buildings were pocked with bullet holes. There was no electricity and no working phone system, as all of the copper wire had been dug up. Any open space had sprouted into either a garbage dump or a refugee camp. An awful odor emanated from the city, a result of the standing refuse, intense heat, and general decay.

"Mogadishu Somalia" — Tales of horror from gangland.

OPPOSITE: After returning from his first trip to Somalia, Dan made this collage for his friend and colleague Aidan Hartley.

NEWSREEL 16: "The Bishop don't come 'round here no more."

Displaced boys.   Ame Camp, Sudan.

Mogadishu Cathedral.

Somalia and
Sudan 1992
July – Aug

Feeding center interviews, Somalia.

The Embassy of the United States
of America, Somalia.

J.M.C. feeds roof singing?

SOMALIA 101

Like many African countries, Somalia is a conglomeration of territories inhabited by different clans who never intended to operate together as one nation. When Somalia gained independence from Britain and Italy in 1960—the two countries with the longest colonial ties to the area—various native leaders took over parts of the country.

In 1969, a military coup d'état left General Siyaad Barre as president of Somalia. Barre was a socialist who associated himself with Lenin. His goal was to modernize the country and, in part, he was successful. Literacy improved from just 5 percent to 55 percent in the decade after he took charge, and many public works programs were initiated.

One of Barre's aims was to get rid of his people's ancient clan system. All Somalis derive from six clans, which are further delineated by subclans. Any allegiance to a government, a workplace, or any other kind of community means nothing compared to a Somali's allegiance to his or her clan. Barre went so far as to outlaw clan loyalty. But he couldn't erase the ancient system; it merely went underground.

Clan tensions simmered beneath the surface throughout the 1980s. In 1988, when Barre finally signed a peace accord with Ethiopia, civil war erupted in northern Somalia. As clan-based guerrilla groups multiplied throughout the rest of the country, with each one claiming its own domain, the dictator tightened his hold on Mogadishu—the only part of the country still fully under his control—bringing Barre the nickname "The Mayor of Mogadishu." The city became Ground Zero for a clan-based civil war, a war that continued even after Barre was ousted from the country and a new henchman, Mohamed Farrah Aidid, became the primary warlord to be feared.

I flew into Mogadishu this time with the Lutherans. These missionary types have hired a huge herculese military transport plane owned by Southern Air Transport and which everyone says is the CIA owned Airline. The pilots looked CIA - real cigar chompers - every one of them looked like George Bush. Other passengers were an old Swedish missionary type lady, and a humourless Irishman. I managed to get my very heavy bag on board and clear my fishy passport through customs.

We land at Mog. Airport. Scorching heat - dragging my enormous suitcase on wobbly wheels through the sand for half a mile. A pair of clueless Turks guarding the gate, one stroking the others leg in a lecherous fashion. I stop a 5 ton U.S. marine transport truck - drive out the gate. little bastard grabs the bag with in head. drive through town people jeering - taunting. Marines at ready. Italians with chickens on their heads. - arrive at embassy compound - carry bag everywhere - finally find some Marines reading playboy. Start selling postcards. Put my stuff in Marines tent roam around selling cards - check in J.I.B. press conference - meet up with irate photographer Jim. see all old hacks. Meet with Canadian Contem. - Room around at night till get busted. starlight scope. Sleep on wooden floor of tent with Marines - Also got caught on razor wire and attempted looting by swarms of nasty little fuckers.

——— Morning airport - French meet the Colonel. big postcard deal - treated very well - lunch - weird French people. cooks. Walked through camp Turks - Zimbabwe Botswana, Italians - arguing. no deal. Little Italian from the South making all kinds of deals. Civilian contractors. Texans, Arabs, Philipinos. disaster construction workers. Do the trash run - hell on earth. Technical graveyard - our AK.47 is confiscated. Marine Corps do General looks under bonnet - New boots for Mr. Elton. reordered postcards. Vienens car is stolen and taken to Bermuda Triangle. district - chopper out to ship - missile launcher weird - inbred - retarded looking sailors - radar room - shopping

139

To arrive in Mogadishu for the first time is like falling into hell.

Dan and Aidan spent their days in Mogadishu visiting feeding centers and aid organizations. Aidid's supporters had destroyed fields and chased farmers from their land. The result was a massive manmade famine. People from the country traveled to Mogadishu in hopes of getting food from UNICEF and other aid groups in secure centers, protected from the warring gunmen who stole food and stockpiled it for themselves. The famine had reached an apex: As many as one thousand people died from starvation every day in Somalia during the summer of 1992.

Dan and Aidan visited Mogadishu's great cathedral, which had been one of the largest churches in Africa until it was set on fire in 1990. There were gaping holes in the immense, towering ceiling, and the steeple had fallen into the road. The heads on the statuary—Jesus, the apostles, and Mary—had been blown off, and some lay shattered at the figures' stone feet. The pews were gone, hacked up for fuel or building materials. The former bishop's body had even been exhumed, his rings and gold teeth scavenged.

Teenagers high on the local drug of choice, *qat*, and carrying AK-47s hung around inside the church, much like kids hanging out on a street corner in the United States. Dan started photographing one at closer range than most photojournalists would usually work. The boy glared at Dan. Aidan urged Dan to put down his camera, but Dan ignored him, much to the more experienced journalist's irritation. The tension was palpable, and Aidan knew things could change for the worse in a second. Dan's

next move surprised everyone. Without taking his eyes off of the gunman, he reached into his camera bag and grabbed the old man mask that he always traveled with. He put it on his head and stuck out his tongue from the greenish rubber face. The teenager was taken aback but then laughed. Dan handed him the mask, and everyone passed it around and took turns wearing it.

explosions — most of
tin roof had b
(they say it sh
grafitti was everyo
shops. Instead

[Dan's] photographs showed he had a tender eye. Don't misunderstand me, he was there for the same reasons I was. To see how it looks and feels. But sooner or later a foreigner had to form a view about the savagery of the Somalis. Were they victims, or were they to blame for their own fate? Most of the foreign correspondents concluded the Somalis were despicable for what they had done to themselves. Dan was different, I suppose because he was young and easygoing. He always treated people decently and looked for what was redeeming about them.

—AIDAN HARTLEY, *THE ZANZIBAR CHEST*

ef Workers safe house.
heavy metal gate
behind us. One of their
shot and the rea
I wanted revenge.
tense as groups of
hed in hushed voices

Mogadishu Cathedral, Somalia

OF WAR IS
DESTRUCTION,
NOT NECESS-
ARILY OF
HUMAN
LIVES
BUT OF
THE
PRODUCTS
OF HUMAN
LABOUR.
WAR IS A WAY
OF SHATTERING TO
PIECES, OR POURING
INTO THE STRATOS-
PHERE, OR SINKING
INTO THE DEPTHS
OF THE OCEAN,
MATERIALS WHICH
MIGHT OTHER-
WISE BE USED
TO MAKE THE
MASSES TOO COMFORT-
ABLE, AND HENCE,
IN THE LONG RUN,
TOO INTELLIGENT
EVEN WHEN
WEAPONS ARE
NOT ACTUALLY
DESTROYED, THE
MANUFACTURE
IS STILL A
CONVENIENT WAY
OF EXPENDING
LABOUR POWER
WITHOUT PRODUCING
ANYTHING THAT
CAN BE CONSUMED.

War, it will be seen not only accomplish the necessary destruction but accomplishes it in a psycologically acceptable way. In principle, it would be easy to waste the surplus labour of the world by building temples and pyramids by digging holes and filling them up again or even producing vast quantities of goods and then setting fire to them. But this would provide only the economic and not the emotional basis for a hierarchical society.

George Orwell, 1984

 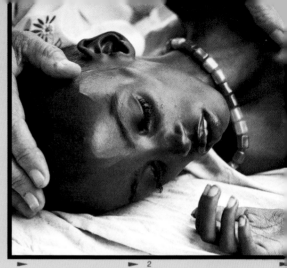

The Sahafi was our home away from home, however grim it was at times. Dan was the cheery, shining personality of the group. If not working in his room that served as an office, you'd find him visiting others, wandering the hallways in *kikoi* and flip-flops or sitting in the stairwell which served as an unofficial congregation point, sunglasses pushing back tousled hair. He was the youngest among us. Many of us were in our thirties, if not forties, and a few above. I never thought of our age difference until after he died. In hindsight, I think he carried in him instinctive wisdom that bridged cultures and generations.

—DONATELLA LORCH, THEN EAST AFRICA BUREAU CHIEF FOR THE *NEW YORK TIMES*

In the coming months, Dan was in and out of Mog on a regular basis as a freelance photojournalist. He got paid fifty dollars a picture from the news agency Reuters—not much, but as one of the agency's youngest photographers, he didn't care about money; he was there for the experience. Although his photos were among the first to expose the severity of the famine and did find their way into newspapers, he, Aidan, and their colleagues continued to fight an uphill battle in gaining attention for Somalia. The war in Bosnia was grabbing most of the foreign coverage, and, as always, the world seemed to shrug at news from Africa. Prince Charles and Princess Diana's failing relationship was far more interesting to Americans.

The practice was for foreign correspondents to work for a few

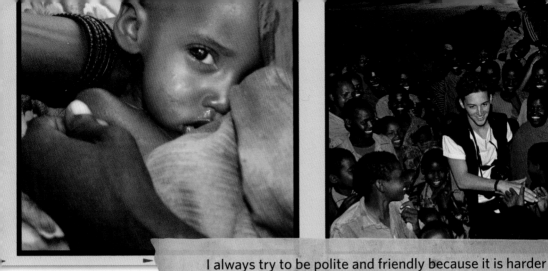

I always try to be polite and friendly because it is harder to shoot at a smiling face. When I do get spotted, the most important challenge is not to show fear.

—DAN ELDON

days at a time and then come out—always to Nairobi, in Dan's case—for a week of recuperation. In order to keep one foot in the "normal" world, journalists needed a reprieve from the constant sound of gunfire and the sight of corpses and emaciated children. For the first few months, Dan lived on adrenaline. He was always eager to get back to Somalia.

He lived in a house rented by Reuters and then at a hotel, the Sahafi, where most of the journalists congregated. Several other photographers took Dan under their wings, teaching him how to develop film in a tiny bathroom rigged as a darkroom, and how to use the T-1 machine that transmitted pictures to Nairobi or London. To rearrange the satellite dish, which often went on the fritz, someone had to hang out of a third-story window.

Dan's photos improved as he received tips and critiques from editors over the phone and studied the work of other photographers. It was a crash course, and he was in heaven.

His years of travel served him well in the field, too, as he figured out the right mix of bluster and deference to carry him through potentially dangerous situations. He was friendly, carrying candy to give to children and sitting down to share mint tea with elders with whom he could talk in a smattering of Swahili and a few words or phrases of Arabic. To make himself look important to the "bang bang" kids—a term the journalists adopted to describe the qat-chewing, gun-happy teenagers who controlled Mogadishu's streets—he carried all sorts of false papers and ID cards, a trick he'd learned from border crossings. Sometimes, though, he found that playing dumb worked best of all.

By October, however, the menacing sights and sounds of Somalia had caught up with Dan psychologically. He decided to take the money he'd earned thus far and go to visit Neema, who had moved to Norway. He'd become increasingly obsessed, covering his room at the Sahafi with images of her. He knew she was dating someone else, but that didn't erase his sureness that they were meant to be together. .

Because of her Somali heritage, he often thought he saw her face. Once, at the hospital, he was unable to photograph a young woman who bore a striking resemblance to Neema but whose hands and feet had been blown off.

When he arrived in Oslo, Neema didn't meet him at the airport. Over and over that week, she ignored him or kept him waiting. Dan sulked around the city, which he found bland and humorless. When they eventually spent time together, it was uneven and con- fusing. They'd be wonderfully tender together, only to fight later.

I feel so lost and destroyed and ashamed to be myself. I try to think of how I used to be just a few weeks ago in Somalia. I could deal with any fear and danger. Even with a crowd of crazed gunmen threaten- ing to kill me, I could calmly ask them for a cigarette. It is a mystery to me how one girl can make me so weak.

—DAN, IN AN UNSENT LETTER TO NEEMA

"Neema Ali"
I love that monster

Dan Eldon"
" I love that Monster

On his way back from Norway, Dan stopped in London for a few days. Spending time with an old family friend, Tara Fitzgerald, he was visibly jittery. It was Guy Fawkes Day, the British equivalent of Halloween, and Dan jerked at the pop and crack of random fireworks. When a car backfired, he reflexively ducked. Tara had never seen her friend frightened before—he had always been the brave one. Now she saw the fear that he lived with in Somalia. Later, they sat in the darkened bedroom with his suitcase. Inside were his photographs of Somalia. "I want to show them to you," he told her, but was incapable of opening the case and removing its contents.

Kathy had been in the United States and returned just before Dan's flight, leaving them only an hour together. Dan brought a pizza, which they ate on the rooftop of Kathy's apartment. They were tense with each other as a result of the series of letters they'd exchanged over the summer. Kathy had inferred that Dan wasn't working hard enough toward supporting himself, and Dan retorted that his mom was prying. He'd written her a formal letter detailing his multiple photography assignments and paychecks. Dan was clearly still smarting. Now, added into the mix, was Kathy's concern for his safety.

There was so much she wanted to ask him, but she also didn't want to open any wounds just before he had to leave. Instead, she listened and thought to herself that they would have more time during his next visit.

On December 9, 1992, the Americans arrived in Mogadishu in full force, to augment the UN's peacekeeping efforts. The journalists who had been covering Somalia for months found their landing at the city's beach to be a farcical media event. The networks flew in high-profile journalists, including anchors who brought along bulletproof vests and stylists to do their hair. On the night of the landing, Dan became a gofer—driving between the beach

LEFT: During what would be their final visit together, Dan and Kathy photographed each other.

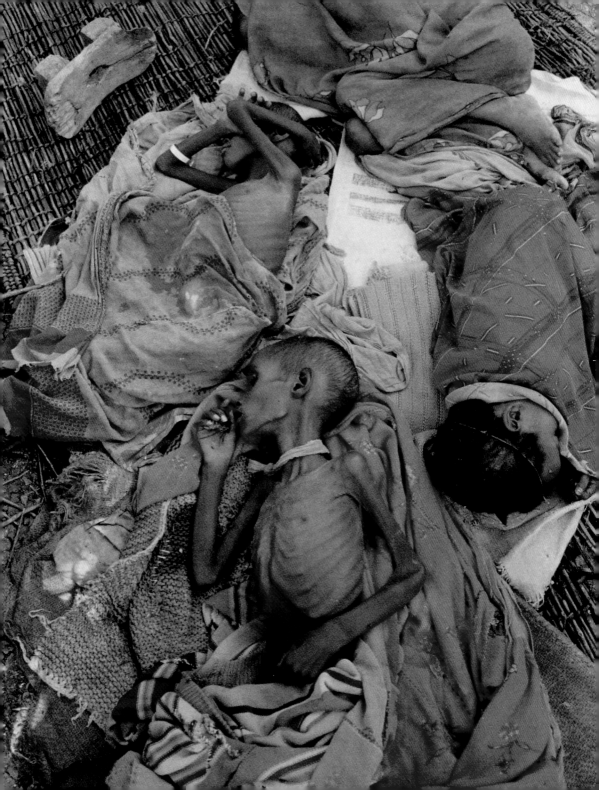

and the Reuters office with equipment. That day, however, he accompanied troops inland to a feeding center in Baidoa—dubbed "The City of Death" because of how many people had starved to death there in previous months. Dan had visited Baidoa many times before, sometimes rising at dawn to photograph the people who had died outside the camp overnight. Now, seeing people getting food—tons and tons of food—without the threat of thugs stealing it, gave him some satisfaction that his work had been worthwhile.

Back home for the holidays, he was relieved to spend time with Amy, his dad, Soiya, and other friends. While visiting the island of Lamu, he wrote several long letters reflecting on the six months he'd just spent in a war zone.

I have been working for Reuters and we had an excellent team and I managed to be quite useful and productive due to my knowledge of the area from having spent quite a good deal of time there was a good feeling being in the middle of a big news story. It felt like all my years of taking silly pictures and making journals of safaris and trips is beginning to bear fruit. But being in that place really eats away at the mind. The shattered bodies and hundreds of walking skeletons really leaves left me changed in a way that I don't even begin to understand myself. I feel like I have to work out who I am and what I like and don't like. Almost from scratch.

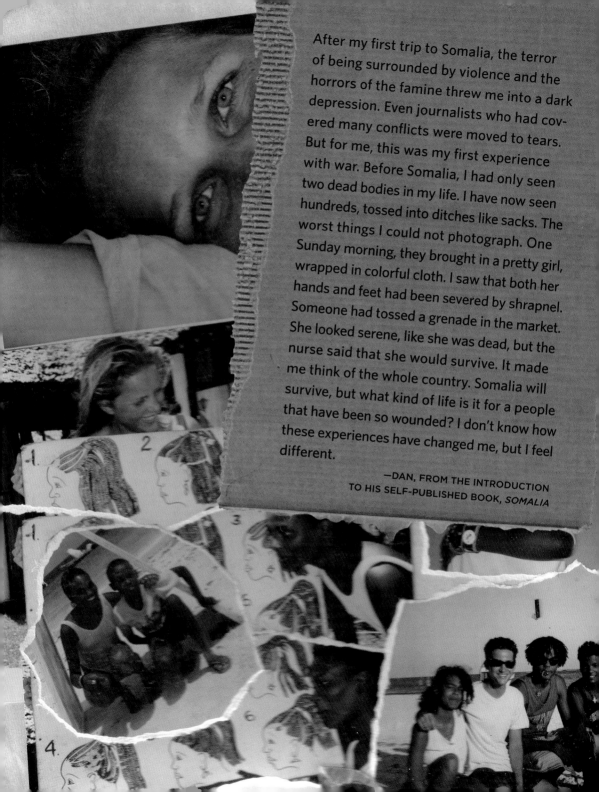

After my first trip to Somalia, the terror of being surrounded by violence and the horrors of the famine threw me into a dark depression. Even journalists who had covered many conflicts were moved to tears. But for me, this was my first experience with war. Before Somalia, I had only seen two dead bodies in my life. I have now seen hundreds, tossed into ditches like sacks. The worst things I could not photograph. One Sunday morning, they brought in a pretty girl, wrapped in colorful cloth. I saw that both her hands and feet had been severed by shrapnel. Someone had tossed a grenade in the market. She looked serene, like she was dead, but the nurse said that she would survive. It made me think of the whole country. Somalia will survive, but what kind of life is it for a people that have been so wounded? I don't know how these experiences have changed me, but I feel different.

—DAN, FROM THE INTRODUCTION TO HIS SELF-PUBLISHED BOOK, *SOMALIA*

ABOVE: Dan and fellow photojournalist Hos Maina with a "technical" in Mogadishu.

Dan returned to Somalia in January with new energy. He started a business making and selling postcards of his photos, and T-shirts with Cobra helicopters printed on them with cheeky sayings like, "I Restored Hope in Somalia." (The American-led project had been called Restore Hope.) He also self-published a book of his photographs. Already well-known and liked by aid workers, Marines, and other military people, Dan was soon filling orders for entire units. He had an entrepreneur's knack for understanding that the Westerners working in Somalia were hungry for something to help their families understand where they'd been.

He did so well that his pockets were routinely stuffed with wads of American dollars and his room at the Sahafi was stashed with boxes of whiskey, garnered in trades with Marines. When he returned to Nairobi, he spent much of his time visiting the print shop to fill new orders. Eventually, he hired his friend Peter Lekarian, a Maasai who was living with Mike at the time, to run the business end from home.

The elation that the Americans' arrival would save the day quickly dissipated. The UN peacekeepers and Americans did nothing to disarm the bands of militia that looted everything and everyone. Landing at the

bombed-out airport, for instance, was an expensive proposition, since anyone from a Red Cross worker to a photographer was hit up for money just to get off the plane. Violence continued, and in time, it actually escalated as Somalis grew tired of all the foreigners. Once the famine abated—in part because of the food aid delivered, but more because it had run its course—many journalists left. Those who stayed holed up in their rooms, fearful of the random violence on the streets.

Dan was one of the few who continued to go out in the city, interacting with local Somalis. The armed guards who drove him around the city and out in the country took to calling him "The Mayor of Mogadishu"—a play on General Barre's nickname but also an acknowledgment of how well liked Dan was.

The most popular spot at the Sahafi hotel was the roof. After dinner—camel meat on pasta and mangoes for dessert—the journalists gathered there to catch a cool breeze from the ocean. Some drank and others chewed qat to combat the stress of the day. They'd talk about what the United States and UN were doing wrong, certain that they could do a better job if they were in charge and then argue about whether Mogadishu or Sarajevo—the sniper-filled capital city of Bosnia—was the more dangerous assignment.

NEXT PAGE: Dan was thrilled when one of his photographs appeared as a double-page spread in *Newsweek*. It was a major success and would help to move him up the pecking order of photographers covering Somalia.

Only five weeks after leaving
Somalia, American forces were
back taking care of unfinished
business. And the Pentagon
was preparing to send 300 U.S.
soldiers on an ill-defined
mission to Bosnia's neighbor,
Macedonia. The rest of the
world still wants Uncle Sam to
play global cop—but is this any
way to do it?

Cry Uncle!

On June 5, 1993, Somalis killed twenty-four Pakistani UN peacekeepers and injured fifty more. The soldiers were conducting a weapons search at Radio Mogadishu, which, in addition to being the warlord Aidid's primary anti-UN propaganda vehicle, was also a weapons site. The dead were horrifically mutilated, indicating the Somalis' growing anger at the foreigners. It was the largest death toll of UN peacekeeping troops in a single event since 1961. The violence was no longer aimed at only whites or the military but at all foreigners, including many black African aid workers and journalists. No one, not even Dan, felt comfortable in Mog anymore.

Dan was increasingly eager to leave Somalia. He wasn't getting much time out of the country and needed a change of scenery. During a trip to Nairobi in June, he talked to his Reuter's bureau chief about a possible reassignment—Bosnia, perhaps. He jotted notes about future safari destinations—Cuba and Nepal—and called Soiya at school, encouraging her to join him for some travel.

While he was home, he spoke with his sister and mother by phone and spent time with his dad, who was recovering from a car accident. He told them all the same thing: He would be fine; he was safe and recognized danger when he saw it. "Don't worry," he'd tell his dad. "I'm in my element."

Back in Mogadishu, Dan found that the city was unusually quiet in early July. He and his fellow journalists were struggling to find a story worth covering. On July 11, Dan headed to a beach that had been taken over by the Americans, complete with suntanners and their own lifeguard. The photos he took of gun-toting female Marines made the papers the next day.

Dan was hanging out on the roof of the Sahafi waiting for a ride to the airport on the morning of July 12. His friend and colleague Hos Maina had just arrived from Kenya to replace Dan, who was headed back to Nairobi for a rest. As several journalists gathered to drink coffee and smoke cigarettes, the quiet of the morning was interrupted by the appearance of several Cobra helicopters buzzing in low circles over a residential area of Mogadishu. For nearly twenty minutes, they fired artillery on one concentrated area. The journalists watched, some taking video or photos, but no one knew what was going on.

After the shooting ended, a car arrived at the front of the hotel and an injured journalist, Scott Peterson, got out. He told of a massive attack on a residential compound, resulting in scores of injured and dead Somalis. "It's getting really dangerous out there," he said as Dan bandaged his arm.

It turned out the Americans believed that the warlord Aidid was in a large Italian-style villa that morning, so they had initiated a bombing campaign in the hopes of killing him. In truth, a group of elders trying to negotiate peace was meeting in the villa. Many women and children were also in the home. As many as seventy people were killed in the attack.

Somalis sometimes came to the Sahafi when they wanted the journalists to cover a specific story. This day was no different. A truck arrived and the Somalis promised the journalists protection. A caravan of five trucks formed. Dan rode along with Reuters colleagues Hos Maina, Shaffi Mohammed, and Anthony Macharia, as well as a German journalist from the Associated Press, Hansi Krause.

Their truck reached the compound first. More than a hundred people from the immediate neighborhood had gathered in the villa's large courtyard to see what had happened. Everywhere, men were piling bloody, horribly burned and mangled bodies into the backs of trucks.

The five journalists quickly and quietly got to work. Instead of fanning out, they remained as a group, working in unison to photograph and videotape the carnage. As Shaffi Mohammad would later remember, they intuitively knew that this situation was different from most they had covered.

They'd been there only a few minutes when a man picked up a stone. "What are you doing here?" he shouted. "The Americans are killing us from above and now they come to take pictures. They work for the Americans!"

The immense grief and horror of the crowd in the courtyard suddenly shifted to anger. "The mood changed in the blink of an eye," Shaffi said later. "'Let's get out of here,' Dan said to me." They turned toward the gate, but it was blocked by pickups, creating a bottleneck. As the crowd swelled, the journalists managed to make their way out into the streets and start running, but by now they were separated, each man going in a different direction.

Bleeding from a stone that had caught him in the head, Shaffi glimpsed Dan and Anthony running ahead of him. Around the next corner, Shaffi found Dan's flak jacket—the heavy, bulletproof vest that would have made it hard for him to run very far. "Smart boy," Shaffi thought.

Dan eventually became separated from Anthony, too. He was surely lost in the city streets, working from instinct. Helicopters still buzzed overhead, and though one pilot saw Dan and radioed for permission to pick up the white man he could see running below, permission was denied. Dan seemed to lose the pack, but upon rounding a corner, he was confronted with a new group coming at him from the opposite direction. With nowhere to turn, he fell to his knees, perhaps hoping to talk his way out of the situation as he had so many times before. Before he could speak, though, the butt of a gun hit the back of his head. He didn't have time to beg or make another plan. He was gone.

"only the dead have
seen the end
of War."

Plato

REPORT OF THE DEATH OF AN AMERICAN CITIZEN ABROAD

American Embassy, Nairobi, Kenya: October 12, 1993
(Post & date of issue)

SSA No..................

ELDON
(Last name)

Name in full ...Daniel Robert Eldon.. Age ..22 years.

Date and Place of Birth...September 18, 1970, London, United Kingdom......

Evidence of U.S. Citizenship U.S. passports #110132246 issued on 11-04-88 at New York and #Z6763926 issued on 10-04-89 at

Address in U.S.A. ....Lilongwe, Malawi.......................................

Permanent or Temporary Address Abroad...P.O. Box 53441, Nairobi, Kenya......

Date of death ....July............12............12............30............1993....
(Month)   (Day)   (Hour)   (Minute)   (Year)

Place of death .(DOA).....42nd Field Hospital......Mogadishu......Somalia
(Number and street) or (Hospital or hotel)   (City)   (Country)

Cause of death...Head Trauma (Cranial cerebral) - M.D. Maj. James J.
(Including authority for statement — if physician, include full name and official title, if any)
Leech's Overseas Certificate of Death .

Disposition of the remains..cremated - ashes scattered......................

Local law governing disinterment of remains provides that..not applicable.......

Disposition of the effects.....family - in possession.........................

Person or official responsible for custody of effects and accounting therefor.............

Mike Eldon (father)...

Traveling/residing abroad with relatives or friends as follows:
NAME   ADDRESS

M. Eldon.................... P.O. Box 53441, Nairobi, Kenya...............

Informed by telegram or telephone (was on assignment for Reuters in Mogadishu)
NAME   ADDRESS   DATE SENT

G. Stewart................... ...Reuters, Cyprus............... ....

Copy of this report sent to:
NAME   ADDRESS   DATE SENT
M. Eldon   P.O. Box 53441
.... 10-12-93 ....
....Nairobi, Kenya............... ....

Notification or copy sent to Federal Agencies: SSA__x__VA_____CSC_____Other_____
(State Agency)
The original copy of this document and information concerning the effects are being placed in the permanent files of the Department of State, Washington, D.C. 20520.

Remarks: U.S. Passports #110132246 & #Z6763926 cancelled and returned to next of kin...

.... (Continue on reverse if necessary.)

Marsha von Baerckheim
(Signature on all copies)

[SEAL]   Consul General   of the United States of America.

DANIEL
(First name)

ROBERT
(Middle name)

JULY 12, 1993
(Date of death)

Additional certified copies available from The Correspondence Branch, Passport Services, Department of State
Washington, D.C. 20524. Each copy $3.00.

☆ U.S. GOVERNMENT PRINTING OFFICE : 1983 0 - 381-526 (8295)

AFTERLIFE

1993–2011

Dan was killed on July 12, 1993, in Mogadishu, ironically by the very people he was trying to help. Three other colleagues—Hos Maina, Hansi Krause, and Anthony Macharia—died that day at the hands of the mob. Of the five in the front truck that entered the villa, only Mohammed Shaffi survived, a bullet having ricocheted off a large video battery pack in his breast pocket.

Dan's life was over, but his spirit was far from gone. Even in her grief, Kathy knew this. At the memorial service a week later, Kathy quoted from "Oh Very Young," one of Dan's favorite songs by Cat Stevens: "You're only dancing on this earth for a short while." She told the crowd, "What Dan would want us all to remember is that you may have only a short while to dance, but you choose your dance. You choose the music for your dance. You dance proudly. You dance loudly. You dance with creativity and vigor, and joy, and most of all you dance with love."

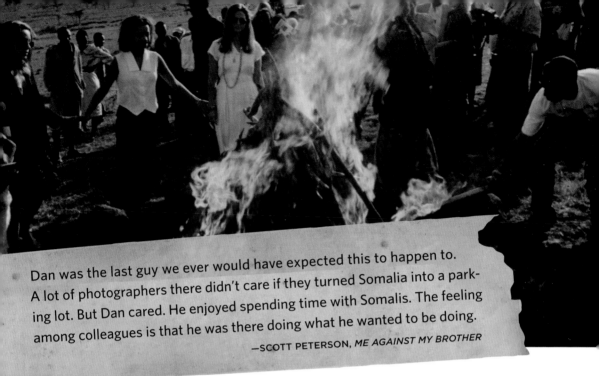

Dan was the last guy we ever would have expected this to happen to. A lot of photographers there didn't care if they turned Somalia into a parking lot. But Dan cared. He enjoyed spending time with Somalis. The feeling among colleagues is that he was there doing what he wanted to be doing.

—SCOTT PETERSON, *ME AGAINST MY BROTHER*

The news of Dan's death circulated slowly. The journalists knew first—they headed to Mike's house before he'd even received official word. That came via a phone call from a senior Reuters manager in Cyprus—initially to let him know that Dan "may" have been killed. Mike simply didn't want to believe what he'd been told and tried— unsuccessfully—to concentrate on business as usual. Another call came a couple of hours later confirming the worst. A fellow journalist had identified the body; it was definitely Dan.

In the days before cell phones or email, it took hours to track down Kathy, who was staying at a hotel in Los Angeles. She finally got the news from her brother-in-law. Then she had to make the most difficult call of her life to Amy, who was beginning an internship in Mexico City.

Many found out from the next day's newspaper. Some, like Hayden Bixby, heard it on the radio. Later, she called Jeff Gettleman and Roko Belic and left a message with Jeff's mom. The two were painting houses that summer and had heard on the radio that some journalists had been killed in Somalia but, like everyone, they assumed it couldn't be Dan. Dan had street smarts. He would be fine. When Jeff returned home late at night, however, he found a slip of paper waiting for him in his mom's handwriting: "Call Hayden." He didn't have to call. He knew.

The "Celebration of Life" ceremony was held a week after Dan's death on Kipenget's land in the Ngong Hills. Family flew in from Iowa and England. Aidan Hartley came from Bosnia, and Soiya Gecaga from London. All of Nairobi turned out, too, or so it seemed. William, who had not worked for the Eldons in several years, appeared on Mike's doorstep just after the news broke and stayed all week, helping to feed people. There were *askaris* who had worked for the Eldons or at ISK, former teachers, friends of Kipenget's, and shop owners and restaurateurs who knew Dan from his trips around Nairobi.

All week, stories surfaced about Dan's many kindnesses. He had quietly been supporting William's family, had lent money to a *matatu* driver in need of a new van, and had given money to his friend Peter Lekarian for driving lessons. He'd taken his old friend Tara Fitzgerald on a difficult and final visit to her childhood home. "We'll buy it back someday and turn it into a disco," he'd told her.

ABOVE: Soiya and Amy lighting the fire at the Celebration of Life ceremony.

People from all periods and parts of his life got up and spoke during the "Celebration of Life," reflecting on Dan's complex personality. Several journalists told stories about his bluster and charm, which they had seen firsthand in Somalia. William described Dan's concern for him, even though he was supposed to be the servant. Lengai, in the midst of exams, couldn't get away from school in England, so Amy read a moving letter he'd written. Then, she and Soiya, along with Dan's old friends and cousins, plunged lit torches into a bonfire. The flame took immediately and burnt wildly as an African choir sang. The next day, Dan's immediate family returned to share stories and spread his ashes into the circle of stones that marked the place where the fire had blazed.

After Dan's death, many of his friends and family grappled with depression and anger. Some of the journalists who had worked with him seriously considered leaving the profession. After trying to return to college in Boston, Amy decided to take a semester off. She worked as a waitress in New York and volunteered on the children's cancer ward of a hospital. At first Kathy was nearly consumed by darkness, but she decided to pour her energy into creating awareness of the risks frontline journalists face. Following a joint memorial for the four men held at St. Bride's Church—the "Journalists' Church" in London—she helped to open an exhibit of their work, which then traveled to ten countries on four continents. Mike

I have never felt so utterly bereft and lost— really an out-of-body experience. My only hope was to transform the horror of what had happened into something positive, so I threw myself into telling people about the challenges faced by frontline journalists like Dan and his colleagues. My emotional turning point came when Amy and I wrote a book, *Angel Catcher: A Journal of Loss and Remembrance,* about our experience of going through grief and arriving at a place of acceptance and peace.

—KATHY ELDON

organized a multimedia exhibition of Dan's art at a gallery in Nairobi and began exploring how to create a living memorial to Dan.

A few weeks after his death, a bag of Dan's belongings from the Sahafi appeared at Mike's house. Amy, Mike, and Donatella Lorch—one of Dan's journalist friends, then with the *New York Times*—went through it together. There were T-shirts of Dan's own design; a pair of cheap Ray-Ban style sunglasses; blue jeans with pocketfuls of dollars from his T-shirt, postcard, and book sales; and a single journal.

The book was newly started, and mostly blank. Dan had glued single photos onto pages without any of the layering and drawings that he usually added. Whether he'd intended to come back and collage them later or whether, at last, he felt his photographs stood alone was unclear.

In the coming months, more of the journals would make their way to Mike's. Dan had left some at Kathy's apartment in London, another at his cousin's in Iowa, and more in Los Angeles with an aunt. Finally, seventeen books—including several he kept as a boy—were collected. Although the family always knew they were special, the journals had been so omnipresent that they didn't always take much notice. Now, however, the books took on new meaning. It was as though Dan still lived through their pages.

Kathy, Mike, and Amy decided the journals should be shared. Although Dan never dreamed of publishing them, it always pleased him when other people admired them. In 1997, Chronicle Books published a compilation of the journals, edited by Annie Barrows, as *The Journey Is the Destination.*

The result was electrifying. The contents of the beat-up books, often thrown in the back of Dezirée, worked on late at night, glued over, or torn up, were suddenly available for anyone to look at and wonder over.

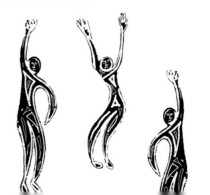

THE JOURNALS

Experiencing Dan's journals is intense for many viewers, as he truly does seem to live in their pages. A swath of his hair is sealed onto a page with red wax. Little faces that appear to be cartoons are, at closer look, made with his thumbprint. There are fingernail clippings, smears of blood, photos of his girlfriends, and countless images of Dan's mischievous, ever-changing face.

Most of the journals began their lives as standard 8½-x-11-inch black blank books found in art supply stores. Dan filled them to overflowing, so many of their bindings are cracked or broken. One book is cinched together with a Moroccan leather belt. Another exists in three separate pieces. Dan didn't create the journals with longevity in mind; they were his laboratory-cum-diary for the present moment. He used delicate and ephemeral materials, including spices and rice, (which bugs have long since eaten); Elmer's glue; eggshells; and tissue-thin papers.

Through these amazing journals, I knew Dan. I felt like I had always known him, that I was called by him for my eye and understanding of the deep waters of emotion that run through life when you have experienced so much intensity at such a young age. I know I wouldn't be able to do this job if I had known him alive, too attached to the man, unable to separate him from the brilliant artist that I feel he is. . . . In short, looking through his journals, I entered a place called heaven. All that troubled me when I was young was finally put to rest. Like so many others I have seen in my gallery, Dan's work on display, they touched my heart and inspired me.

— LISA CANDELA, GALLERY OWNER AND PHOTOGRAPHER

ABOVE: Fellow journalist Donatella Lorch celebrates with kids at the CURA orphanage near Nairobi.

In 1994, on what would have been his son's twenty-fourth birthday, Mike and his soon-to-be wife, Evelyn Mungai, started The Dan Eldon Place Of Tomorrow, or The DEPOT in Nairobi. The idea was to keep Dan's memory and spirit alive through an outdoor leadership development center for young people. Its motto, *Inspiring you to fulfill your potential*, has since moved tens of thousands of people.

The DEPOT commemorated something Dan said to his father one day—that his bedroom didn't really need to be cleaned up because it was merely his "depot," the place where he stored his things and occasionally slept. A friend noticed that the first two letters of *depot* were Dan's initials. Mike then had to find words for the remaining letters. "Place Of" came to him; he then turned to the dictionary, where he went through all the words beginning with *t*. The one he liked best was *Tomorrow*.

Although The DEPOT started by serving young people—high school and university students, street children, the mentally challenged, you name it—their programs have grown to include people from all kinds of organizations, from banks to manufacturing companies, from government ministries to rural communities, from the World Bank to the UN. At The DEPOT, everyone learns how to express their energy and align it with others, as team members and leaders...just as Dan did.

The Ford Foundation supports an annual Youth Leadership and Citizenship program at The DEPOT, attracting young people from around East Africa, and the Peace Corps ran a two-week event for the deaf there. The DEPOT has become a full-fledged consulting firm and Mike Eldon's life's work, all thanks to Dan.

A year after Dan's death, five journalists loaded up Dan's Land Rover from the Morocco

ABOVE: The Dan Eldon Place of Tomorrow.

ABOVE: Children at an orphanage in Croatia standing in front of Big Blue.

trip, Big Blue, with toys and drove her from London to an orphanage in Croatia.

Amy had returned to work on her undergraduate degree in communications from Boston University, and she started working on a project about journalists in war zones. "After Dan's death, I'd learned so much more about journalists who sacrifice their lives to tell important stories; some of them literally die to tell the story. After I wrote a treatment for a class (and got a B+!), my mom and I had the chance to present it to Turner Broadcasting. Miraculously, it was green-lit in three days."

When The DEPOT was launched in 1994 we never imagined it would spread Dan's spirit to so many, and so powerfully. By now over twenty-five thousand people have passed through our programs. We love what we do, every day of it, as we strengthen and uplift the huge variety of men and women with whom we engage. They love it too, and not least when they hear about Dan and the way he lived his life—which they always do. We work with all kinds of groups, the young and the not-so-young. But at whatever age, at whatever level, we bring out the child within each one.

I also never imagined that a time would come when my work with The DEPOT would occupy all of my time, as it has done for the last few years. I'm thrilled to be inspired by my son, and to honor him, in everything that I do.

—MIKE ELDON

In 1997, Amy, Kathy, and a production team spent several months shooting and editing the two-hour documentary *Dying to Tell the Story,* which features seven of the world's top frontline journalists, including reporter Christiane Amanpour and photographer Don McCullin. It was nominated for an Emmy, as well as other major industry awards.

During filming, they flew into Mogadishu, still a very dangerous place. They were ushered through a bombed-out airport some thirty miles out of town, leaving them only a few hours on the ground. Mohammed Shaffi, the one survivor from the July 12 attack, accompanied Amy and Kathy to the Sahafi hotel and then on to the villa, a burnt-out husk, where the violence had begun on July 12.

Following Dan's death, Kathy spent increasingly long periods in Los Angeles, eventually buying an apartment there and making it

her home. In 1998, she launched the Creative Visions Foundation to help other creative activists like Dan use film, photography, and art to ignite positive change in the world.

As more people heard Dan's story, they would often contact Kathy and share their own dreams with her. "Many of them were inspired—on fire with their ideas," she says, "but they weren't sure where to begin. Creative Visions helps them by providing tools and resources to transform ideas into action. We're like a big, safe but exciting tent from which to grow. It's been such an amazing thing to watch fledgling programs thrive after getting their start with us."

One young woman who came to Kathy seeking guidance reminded her quite a bit of Dan. Jessica Mayberry was a recent college graduate who had been working on various TV shows in the late 1990s. Although they were

ABOVE: Kathy and Amy spent one harrowing and emotional day in Mogadishu in 1997 while filming *Dying to Tell the Story.*

decent jobs by many standards, she felt unfulfilled. Eager to help impoverished people use the power of media, she envisioned an organization that could serve as a media network for people who earn less than two dollars a day. In 2002, Kathy encouraged her to start Video Volunteers.

Today, her organization supports a network of community video filmmakers in India who produce videos focusing on local issues that range from health and human rights to child marriage and water access.

Over the past ten years, the Creative Visions Foundation has supported more than eighty projects and productions by creative activists on four continents.

Going to Somalia was frightening because anarchy still ruled in Mogadishu. It lacks any kind of infrastructure and is controlled by whoever has the most guns. Being at the villa was surreal. As we stepped through the debris that still littered the inside of the house, I could almost hear the sounds of the women serving the elders before the mortars hit. I was haunted by the death and destruction that took place in that compound. As we left, women in long, bright dresses surrounded our van and pounded on it angrily, demanding that we leave. Our guide said they didn't want to be reminded of the horror of that day when they, too, lost brothers and fathers, mothers and sisters.

—KATHY ELDON

ABOVE: The Creative Visions Team, 2011.

ABOVE: Kathy on Safari in Uganda, 2002.

ABOVE: In South Africa, Amy toured Nelson Mandela's former prison cell with Ahmed Kathrada, who had been an inmate with the eventual South African president and antiapartheid leader.

When working on the documentary *Dying to Tell the Story*, Amy came up with the term "peace correspondent." If Dan and his colleagues were often called war correspondents, then why not have a group of journalists who covered peace? She initiated two projects that celebrated young people working to make a difference in their immediate worlds.

The first project, *Soldiers of Peace*, documented the Children's Peace Movement in Colombia through the eyes of five teenagers who had experienced the violence of their country's civil war. The group presented their message to the Hague Appeal for Peace and became powerful spokespeople for peace in the world.

Wanting to tell more stories of young people actively working to change debilitating conditions in their neighborhoods, states, countries, and beyond, Amy and Kathy produced a PBS series in 2003 called *Global Tribe*. Amy hosted and traveled to the Philippines, South Africa, and Mexico, meeting with young activists and learning about how they dealt with challenges.

Texas journalism teacher Wynette Jameson saw *Dying to Tell the Story* when it first came out in 1998. She's used it in her classroom ever since. The first year, she had all the students write postcards to Amy, and to their surprise, Amy handwrote a response to each of them.

To borrow the words of Joseph Campbell, I'd say people are drawn to Dan's story because there is such a dearth of "literature of the spirit." We're inundated with the news of the day, celebrity gossip, and many other superficial stories, but we lack stories that illuminate the eternal. Dan's story achieves that—he reminds us that we're more than the body that we prize, or perhaps the one that's fraying and falling away— we are the spirit within. His journey beautifully recalls the universal—that we live, we die. And what we do in between is evanescent.

When we look at Dan's life, I suspect in some ways, we don't necessarily see Dan. We see ourselves. There he is. Dan in Dezirée, windswept, framed against blue sky and possibility, and we say to ourselves, "That's me." Dan is the mirror. It's as if we see ourselves clearly for the first time. For an instant, it's not Dan in Dezirée. It's me. Dan is the voice in your own head. The whisper that coaxes: "You can do this"— *this* being whatever dream lies embedded in that person's heart. So, we roll down the Mississippi on a barge, like we've always dreamed of. We quit our job as a UPS guy and pick up a camera and make that documentary halfway around the world. We go to Uganda to help rescue child soldiers and end up starting a movement to end a full-scale war. Dan's story is a tremendous example of the power of example. He calls up what we know inside to be true.

—PATTY KIM, DIRECTOR OF *DESTINY*, A DOCUMENTARY ABOUT DAN ELDON

ABOVE: Jason Russell, left, filming with two other members of the Invisible Children team.

Dan's story, as well as Kathy's and Amy's work, are now mainstays in Jameson's classroom. Dan, she says, "teaches himself," and his story has inspired an entire generation of Texas students. One of them, Micah Wesley, met Kathy Eldon when she was a sophomore in Jameson's journalism class. When Kathy came to visit, Micah learned about various programs sponsored by Creative Visions, including the Strong Heart Fellowship Program, which provides safety and guidance to young people affected by Liberia's civil war. The next summer, Micah interned for the founder of Strong Heart. Then she got involved with Invisible Children, a student-run organization originally inspired by Dan that is dedicated to bringing peace to Northern Uganda.

ABOVE: Kathy works with high school journalists and teacher Wynette Jameson (far right).

ABOVE: Loretta, a refugee from Liberia, with her mentor, Michah Wesley.

Now Micah is working toward a degree in community development, with the hope of being on the ground in Liberia in the near future. She says that everything she's gotten involved with has had Dan as its root inspiration. "Dan is the top of the pyramid. There are so many people who were touched by his story and then by Kathy and Amy's work—Strong Heart and Invisible Children are only two of many; the list just keeps going. And I want to be on that list! I want to be able to say that Dan was the source!"

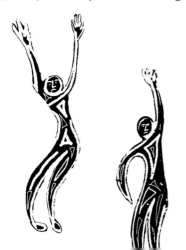

I dare you to find another individual in their life who was able to jump first and fear later. Who else could roll into an African village, have everyone fall deeply in love with him, dance, play, laugh, and take compelling photographs, then be off on the next safari while somehow leaving a part of himself behind? In everything I create, I think of Dan. His influence runs throughout all the stories I tell.

—JASON RUSSELL, COFOUNDER OF
INVISIBLE CHILDREN

EIJI SHIMIZU, "DAN," ROKO BELIC   JEFFREY GETTLEMAN   HAYDEN BIXBY   RYAN BIXBY

People who knew Dan well were, of course, the most changed by his presence. Childhood friends like Soiya Gecaga, Marilyn Kelly, and Tara Fitzgerald have all gone on to work with aid organizations in Africa. Most of the members of STA have been significantly affected by their trip and time with Dan. Given that they came together so randomly, a self-selected, ragtag group who each learned about STA in his or her own way, they have gone on to do amazing things as a whole. Robert Gobright is unaccounted for, but most of the group stays in close touch.

In 1999, **Roko Belic** and his brother produced *Genghis Blues,* a documentary that follows the journey of blind American singer Paul Pena to the isolated Asian nation of Tuva to compete in the Tuvan throat singing competition. The film was nominated for an Academy Award. Currently, Roko is working with **Eiji Shimizu** on a documentary about happiness. In addition to the film, Eiji publishes biography-like graphic novels in order to spread positive messages around the world. The series includes the life stories of the fourteenth Dalai Lama, Mother Teresa, Che Guevara, Mahatma Gandhi, Aung San Suu Kyi, and others. He hopes there will be a book about Dan in the series eventually.

Hayden Bixby is an English professor at Edmonds Community College north of Seattle. She and her partner have founded a service-learning program in conjunction with the Cura Orphanage outside Nairobi, started by Mike Eldon and his wife, Evelyn. Cura is home to fifty children who have lost their parents to AIDS.

After graduating from college with a degree in geology, **Ryan Bixby** joined an environmental consulting company near Seattle, where he is currently the chief operating officer. He and his wife have two children and spend a lot of time with his sister, Hayden, and her family.

AMY ELDON TURTELTAUB

MARTE RAMBORG

ELINOR TATUM

Lengai Croze lives with his wife and children in Scotland, where he works as an architect. His family still lives outside of Nairobi near the gorge where Dan loved playing so much.

Jeffrey Gettleman works for the *New York Times* as the East Africa bureau chief. He covers twelve countries and has focused much of his work on internal conflicts in Kenya, Congo, Somalia, Sudan, and Ethiopia. He lives in Nairobi with his wife and son.

Lorraine Govinden is raising her two young sons in Southern California and studying to become a master herbalist.

Akiko Tomioka Miyamoto lives in Tokyo with her son, Kotaru, and works with Japan Airlines.

In 2008, **Amy Eldon Turteltaub** became a mom. Her first son was born just a day after Dan's birthday; her second son, Daniel, was born in spring 2010. She works closely with her mother as the executive vice president of Creative Visions Foundation and lives in Los Angeles with her husband, a film director.

Christopher Nolan is a film director whose works include *The Dark Knight, Batman Begins, Memento,* and *Inception*. He and his wife, Emma Thomas, who has produced most of his films, have three children and live near Los Angeles.

Marte Ramborg traveled the world while working for the Norwegian Red Cross before having children and settling on her family's small farm outside of Oslo. She now works as director of the communications department for the Norwegian Air Ambulance. Her parents continue to live in Nairobi.

Elinor Tatum became the editor in chief of the *New York Amsterdam News,* the oldest and largest black newspaper in New York City, when she was twenty-seven. She is now publisher and serves on the Creative Visions Foundation board.

As with most families who have lost a loved one, the Eldons still mourn Dan and each of them has moments of disbelief that he is no longer here. Yet he is present in remarkable ways. His art and life have inspired countless others to go on their own journeys, sometimes giving up jobs or interrupting studies to do something completely different. Several, like Jason Russell, cofounder of Invisible Children, have started nonprofits that have had profound effects on the lives of thousands. Some friends work in Africa—especially Kenya and the still-impoverished Somalia—trying to improve the lives of the children Dan loved so much. Donatella Lorch, a fellow journalist, is working with UNICEF in East Africa on girls' issues and volunteers at the Cura Orphanage.

Among Dan's favorite aphorisms was "Seek clarity of vision." Many people who knew him—and even those who have come to know him through his work—sensed that Dan had a clearer vision than most of us. The way in which he managed to follow his dreams so boldly and directly, even in such a short life, suggests that he knew something many of us don't—that he tapped into a very deep source.

While others buy self-help books, exercise, take drugs, or go to therapy, Dan sought answers on a pitted road in southern Tanzania, and in a sweaty hotel lounge in Casablanca. He sought answers on the Mexican-U.S. border and over sweetened mint tea in bombed-out homes in Mogadishu. What he might have done with the answers he found, we'll never know. Some believe he would have gone back to school and would be making films now; others think he would have stayed with journalism awhile longer but ultimately moved into some kind of aid work. Either way, art would have remained a constant. What we do know is that Dan is a spark, the suggestion of what a life lived to the fullest might look like. He is the inspiration, not the destination.

Dan Eldon

DEZIREE SAFARIS

Team Deziree "Free at last" Voyages - The Search for clean water in a swamp

"Energy, sincerity, clarity of vision, creativity"

Mission Statement for... Safari as a Way of Life.

"To explore the unknown and the familiar, distant and near, ~ look for solutions - not problems ~ and to record in detail with the eyes of a child, any beauty, (of the flesh or otherwise) horror, irony, traces of utopia or Hell. Select your team with care, but when in doubt, take on new crew and give them a chance. But avoid at all costs fluctuations of sincerity with your best people."

It is therapeutic to apply a well bored beautiful naked body onto ones own flesh at least twice a day in tropical or non tropical climes.

The most important part of vehicle maintainance is clean windscreen so if you are broken down you will enjoy the beauty of the view.

NOTE: There is little difference between being lost and exploring.

create. Avoid eating nasty food when the taste can easily be improved by sauces. It is foolish and hazardous not to dance in Africa, some sauces and clean water.

Also, ensure that electronic devices to play music are properly serviced. The more music you like the happier you will be.

New York London Nairobi Rome Yokohama Paris

RESOURCES

If you are inspired by Dan Eldon's story to become an artist, adventurer, or creative activist, here are some ways that you can get involved and make a difference—whether in your neighborhood, town, state, country, or around the world!

DANELDON.ORG

CREATIVEVISIONS.ORG

DANELDON.COM

THEONREVOLUTION.ORG

INVISIBLECHILDREN.COM

ACKNOWLEDGMENTS

Any work about Dan Eldon is possible only through the generous spirit of his family—Kathy, Amy, and Mike Eldon—who have shared their son's story, his journals, and so many family artifacts with me and others who wish to extend his life to a larger audience. Dozens of Dan's friends have also been very kind in sharing their memories. Some who dug especially deep, going through old photo albums and working hard to recall dates, places, and names from decades ago, include Eiji Shimizu, Long Westerlund, Eric Taylor, Marte Ramborg, Donatella Lorch, Hayden Bixby, and Nicola Graydon.

The mechanics of this book have not been without their challenges. Putting it all together has been the hard work of a team of exceptionally patient people: Joey Borgogna, Kat Fowler, Jessica Lapham, Kelly Sims, Beth Abrahamson, and Lisa Candela. The gurus at Digital Fusion in Los Angeles have been instrumental—Christine Olsen for her attention to detail and Hugh Milstein for his generosity and vision.

This book was in many ways the brainchild of its editor, Julie Romeis, who has shepherded it (and me) through thick and thin. Her exceptional good cheer never faltered.

Finally, among those who aided me personally as I worked on this project, I was buoyed by the love and support of Barb Groth, Jenn Shreve, Alan Rapp, Chris Loeckle, and especially my children, Bella and Tobey—the best cheerer-uppers there ever were!

Jennifer New is the author of *Dan Eldon: The Art of Life* as well as *Drawing from Life: The Journal as Art*. She has delved deeply into Dan's life through his art and journals and talked extensively with family and friends. She lives in Iowa City, Iowa, with her two children.